I'M NOT MAD I'M JUST IN MY FEELINGS

STUDY GUIDE:
Social and Emotional Similarities
that Connect and Predict Past,
Present, and Future Outcomes

Dr. Lawrence V. Bolar

authorHOUSE®

AuthorHouse™
1663 Liberty Drive
Bloomington, IN 47403
www.authorhouse.com
Phone: 833-262-8899

Published by AuthorHouse 06/10/2021

ISBN: 978-1-6655-2656-2 (sc)
ISBN: 978-1-6655-2655-5 (e)

Library of Congress Control Number: 2021910142

Print information available on the last page.

Any people depicted in stock imagery provided by Getty Images are models, and such images are being used for illustrative purposes only. Certain stock imagery © Getty Images.

This book is printed on acid-free paper.

DEDICATION PAGE

This book is dedicated to Dr. Dimitri Bradley and the many lessons I gleam from his ministry, life and journey. The book in essence is the answer or response to his book, <u>U Mad?</u>. I have listened to his messages on various occasions and some of his teaching series. His creative style of articulating the word of God has motivated me beyond measure. His charismatic approach based on my experience is only parallel to his creative teaching and extremely unique style of dress. A man of God with many gifts and talents that has inspired thousands to live a more productive and successful life in God. Dr. Bradley's Life and Death were filled with blessings that have yet to be told or manifested.

CONTENTS

ABSTRACT

SCHEMES, SCANDALS, BETRAYALS, DEBAUCHERLY, LIES and MURDER

The book is designed to provide each reader the opportunity to explore the lives of men and women of the bible and see themselves in similar situations and circumstances. The book will give insight on the Old Testament's characters, lives, emotions and outcomes. The book gives various insights and points to consider while reading from the author's expert opinions.

BOOK PURPOSE

I am writing this book with great excitement and compassion. In addition, I am writing the book with the specific purpose of teaching and learning in mind. I recognize the importance of gaining additional insight and understanding on why we do what we do and the significance of it. In understanding who we are we must gain knowledge of our ancestors and learn from their examples and lived experiences. The lived experiences I will highlight here will come from the word of God, specifically the Old Testament. I have often heard people say I do not like or understand reading the Old Testament portion of the bible. Well, it is my goal to bring the Old Testament to life for you. I believe that it is the Old Testament that gives life to the New Testament. I further believe there is a need to study them both because without the understanding of them both a secure balance in life cannot be obtained. I love reading studying and learning about the scriptures. I have learned from many mentors and heard the scriptures taught and preached close to four decades. I am still learning today and there is still so much more for me to learn. My goal is to take some of the incredibly unique and specific teachings and stories from the Old Testament and make them more practical for the reader to understand and learn. I will include lots of scriptures as references and offer some prospective from my point of view. Sit back, relax and let us fly this jet together.

BACKDROP/FRAMEWORK

Differences Between Emotions and Feelings

I decided that it was extremely important that before we go to deep into the textual concepts that it is that we have some basic understanding on what emotions and feelings are. Knowing the differences between emotions and feelings is not a mere epistemological or linguistic exercise; it will help us to better understand our reactions and behaviors, allowing us to regulate our affective responses to achieve a greater level of understanding and well-being.

What are emotions? Emotions are reactions of affective valence before certain stimuli, which can be external, something that we see or live, or internal, as a thought or a memory. Emotions unleash a set of hormonal and neurochemical responses that produce a state of activation, impelling us to immediate action.

What are feelings? Feelings generate the same physiological and psychological responses as emotions, but have a conscious evaluation incorporated. They involve the awareness and appreciation of emotion and the affective experience that we are living.

Therefore, the main differences between emotions and feelings are:

1. **Duration.** Emotions are transient states that come and go relatively quickly. Feelings, on the other hand, are more stable affective states over time. Joy, for example, is an emotion, while love is a feeling.

2. **Order of appearance.** Feelings are the result of the emotions, so that usually precede them. Joy, for example, can be transformed into happiness and attraction into love.
3. **Intensity.** Emotions are usually more intense than feelings since their main objective is to predispose us to action. The complex processes of assessment that usually intervene in the feelings subtract a little intensity.
4. **Processing level.** Emotions are given unconsciously, generating an almost immediate response, while feelings, by demanding more time for their formation, are processed in a conscious manner.
5. **Degree of regulation.** Emotions are affective states difficult to control because they generate automatic psychophysiological reactions. We cannot completely contain emotions such as fear or joy, for example, and as soon as we experience them, they will manifest through micro expressions. Feelings, on the contrary, can be better managed over time, looking for strategies to express them in a more assertive way.

However, emotions and feelings are often difficult to separate in practice because where there is a feeling there are usually different emotions and vice versa.

Understanding the differences between emotions and feelings helps us, however, not to feel guilty for our first emotional reactions. It also teaches us not to cling to them, so that those unpleasant can disappear as naturally as they have appeared.

How many emotions are out there?

In psychology there is a consensus that refers to 6 types of basic emotions: fear, anger, disgust, sadness, surprise and joy. However, recent research has shown that humans face and can create more than 7,000 different expressions that reflect a wide range of emotions.

Therefore, basic emotions are simply the basis for building more subtle and complex feelings and emotions that blur our experiences.

CHAPTER 1

LEARNING HOW TO MANAGE
MY FEELINGS

If there is one thing I have learned in this life, that is everyone gets into their feelings from time to time. In fact, getting into your feelings happens without warning most of the time. Someone either does something or say something that sparks a defensive emotion inside of you that catches you completely off guard. Once this happens instantly your mind is captured and your attention is immediately arrested. Your thoughts, and your body language shifts from one state of being to a totally different state of being or thinking. The interesting thing is that rarely does anyone want to ever admit that they are actually in their feelings. This all happens in a matter of seconds and before you know it you have potentially said or done something you regret. I know when I'm getting into my feelings the majority of the time but for some strange reason it's just so hard to admit to being in your feelings. I believe it's largely due to our pride and refusal to be vulnerable to others. So typically we lie and say we are not into our feelings or we simply just deny, deny deny.

Getting into one's feelings is totally unavoidable regardless of your gender, title, or social economic status. No one is totally exempt, be it the President of the United States, the church pastor or the AAU coach. No matter the title or position it happens from the least of them to the greatest of them. So my objective with this book is to show the similarities of how much all of us have in common. These commonalities didn't just happen but they started from the very beginning of time. I plan to unpack these unique discoveries and teach you some very interesting biblical facts. For example, remember the birth of baby Jesus and that whole story. Let me refresh your memory on the gossip. Mary tells her future husband that she is pregnant and oh by the way the baby is not yours it's the Lords. I don't care how spiritual you may be, this is a hard pill to swallow. Think of the scandal and the gossip this entire dynamic creates. Think about it for a second, can you imagine being in Joseph, Jesus step father's mind for a second when he had to face his family and friends and tell them Mary the mother of Jesus was pregnant and the baby wasn't his but the Lords? Think about your own family for a second and how they would respond. You already know everyone in the family is not a Christian and definitely not saved if you understand what that really means. For all intense purposes everyone knows Mary to be a virgin. Joseph knows that he has never had sex with her. So, how does this all happen? Why should he believe her? He might not be mad but he definitely is in his feelings about her current situation.

Interesting right, and you probably never thought about it. The Bible doesn't mention much however it did mention how he had planned to privately put her away. These were his exact thoughts before an angel of the Lord revealed to him that the baby was truly of the Holy Spirit. The angle even shared with Joseph that his name would be called Jesus in Matthew 1:18-25.

So we can imagine Joseph was in his feelings because he was going to privately divorce her. This means for both of their names sake and their family names he was going to go through with the wedding, however he was definitely going to divorce her privately. To be honest who could blame him? I don't I would have done the same thing unless an angel of the Lord had come to me.

See how easy a person can get into their feelings and this happens no matter your age. Joseph was 90 years old at the time. I bet you didn't know that either but when he found out that the young woman name Mary Jesus's soon to be mom was pregnant before he was to marry her and be with her he was definitely about to back out of that marriage quickly. I know now you're thinking Joseph was entirely too old to be marrying her anyway. Do you see how you just got into your feelings finding out that Joseph was potentially in his 90's? We really don't know how old he was because the bible doesn't make mention of his age or his death. We do know that he stepped up and became Jesus's adoptive father on earth. Now it was custom for older men to marry younger women but Joseph clearly wasn't desperate enough to marry Mary even though he was older than her. The point to consider is that although he initially got in his feelings about the news, he still did the right thing and you perhaps learned a little more about Mary and Joseph than you knew before reading this book. I started the book off with an example of a male because as men we like to think it's only women who get emotional, especially during the female monthly cycle stages. I have been in enough relationships in my lifetime, to know that as a man we stay in our feelings all the time. This book will be very intentional about connecting current day emotions to past emotional highlights of biblical characters.

I am not mad; I am just in my feelings is a must read. I believe it will change your life. In fact, I am confident that this book will change your life for several reasons. I believe if you are honest with yourself you will realize that. There are so many things that are taking place right now in our world that we simple just do not understand and cannot be explained by man or by human explanation. In fact, I am writing this book in the middle of a National Pandemic, an economic crisis and a war on racism in America. If there were ever a time in life, we needed understanding and clarity about our existence and or why we do what we do it is now.

The whole world is in their feelings based on fear, pain, and hurt.

Especially when comes to topics such as religion, relationships, and politics. Think about this little fact, our President, President Trump will step down from the oval office and fight, argue, dispute or entertaining the craziest things through his twitter account. Now if that is not crazy or an example of people being in their feeling, I do not know what is? Social media is at an all-time high and low based on people being in their feelings. Think about it, people feel extremely comfortable blasting each other over Facebook, Instagram or Twitter. People are saying and admitting things that they would have never said or done face to face. There are people you have known for years and as a result of where we are in our world they are saying and doing peculiar things and I do not mean that peculiar in a good way. There has never been a time in my lifetime where the country has been more divided on so many topics and levels. We see the president of the United States causing more confusion and chaos than we have ever seen before. The position of United States President is an extremely powerful position. The position is normally held by someone who appears to be more stable. In addition, not a position of such instability! There are pastors ranting and raving about if you are a democratic voter you are going to hell. There is such chaos and confusion going on in our people and our world like never seen before. In simple terms people are really in their feelings. People being in their feeling is not anything new per say, but it is heightened on a much larger scale today. The unique thing is, people will say, I am not mad although in their demeanor they appear to be mad or sound mad.

The world is in utter chaos through fear and pain. Although pain is one of the midwives of purpose. I say that because there is a certain amount of pain needed to cause growth. I love a famous quote by Frederick Douglas a former slave he stated, "Without Struggle there can be No Progress". I love this quote and I have lived by it ever since I embraced it. I strongly believe out of great pain comes greatness even if while you were in pain you were in your feelings. Feeling are feelings some good some not so good. Whatever your feelings maybe just be honest with oneself and others. You may be saying one thing but presenting something totally different.

This book will be pack filled with loads of information. For example, this book will, address your pain your emotions and provide a causal comparative analysis to people and our society today in comparison to biblical characters of the pass. You think reality T.V is filled with drama and chaos just wait until we unfold the life of some of the greatest biblical characters you have ever known of. I know that some of the information that I will share with you will be hidden treasures you may have never heard of or thought of from this prospective. You will see examples of people you have been taught about for years but never really knew the ends and out of. The book will share and show you hidden things that you never knew or notice or perhaps no one ever exposed you to.

To me, I believe this has been a defining year. 2020 is definably the year that our world as we once knew it changed significantly due to death defying diseases, tragic murders and political chaos. We are at a time in this life were the entire worlds emotions and feelings are all over the place. To give you a little back drop we are in the middle of COVID-19, the Corona Virus and the country is divided based on racism and politics. This is a bloody potion that must be dealt with strategically and methodically through and by the word of God through the Holy Scriptures. I love studying the bible and comparing our life to the life of characters of the past. I do not expect everyone to agree with my opinions and philosophy however, I do want to intrigue you to the point that you study for yourself.

Our country is in the middle of civil unrest with racial protesting all over the world, to include rioting and looting. George Floyd has been killed by a Caucasian male police officer. Something that has been happening for decades and people are furious. The officer killed him by placing his knee on his neck. This happened all while in handcuffs as the world watches it on video. I am not mad I am just in my feelings because it is not that this is new it is just that we are living in an age where the video camera is available at our fingertips and social media is available. Social media has become one of the largest displays of information around the world today. Social media allows the world to see some of the very ugly things that has taken place in the life of African Americans for decades. There are many pressing things going on in our world today however none as pressing today than racism. The unfortunate thing is we see our nation being turned upside down in a way we have never seen it before. We have a President by the name of Trump who is very controversial to say the least who has not created order but supreme uneasiness and confusion. I believe if there was ever a time, we need clarity and understanding now is that time. Now is not the time to get distracted in all the chaos or madness that we see on our social media accounts, CNN or Fox New reports. Now is a time to develop prospective with clarity and understanding. How many of you know that God is not an author of confusion? However, he can operate under any all circumstances.

Learning how to manage my emotions/ feelings by using the word of God. This book will be based on the life of some of Gods most popular and influential characters and chosen people. The goal is to provide you with the opportunity to see that we are not so far removed from the people in the bible. In my experiences, often time we feel like we cannot relate to the Bible or the people in the bible. I disagree with that view point. In my personal opinion, I believe the bible is one of the most interesting and most relevant historical vantage points that we can use today. Once we see just how much we have in common with the people we have heard so much about and even place on pedestal, the better we will be able to build on our relationship with God. Relationships are complicated only if we make it and are not willing to be open, honest, and transparent with one another about our true feeling and viewpoint. Being open and honest about our individual viewpoints and feelings allows growth to take place. The growth can take place by exposing our inner thoughts, asking the questions that are embarrassing or in our opinion complicated in our minds.

I believe the bible is very misunderstood and often viewed as complicated to read or understand. I don't disagree with that in totality. The reason being is because you do have to have a certain level of anointing to understand some of the deeper meanings and hidden concepts that the bible reveals. So please do not misunderstand me.

The purpose of this book. *I am Not Mad*, I am just in my feelings. I want to show you that there are many phenomenal stories and even dramatic scenes in the bible that you may not have even seen in the bible that you may not have ever uncovered or realized that was there.

CHAPTER 2

FIRST FAMILY DRAMA

I am Not Mad; I am just in my feelings is so real, but so complicated. I plan to take you all the way back to the beginning of time to prove to you just how real this is. Let me explain by giving you some biblical examples. Some of this information may be new to some and a refresher course to others. I will make special reference to some distinctive lessons that can be learned rather easy, but it does take additional research and studying on the part of each reader. The additional research and studying will help because you will see and perhaps think on a much higher level.

My goal is to use biblical examples as God leads me to do so. My first stop on this journey is the drama between Adam and Eve. You think that reality T. V. is filled with suspense and drama just wait and see how much more exciting reading and studying the word of God is.

So, as we enter this scene, we discover that even from the very beginning of time men and women have always been caught up in their emotions and feelings. This started happening way before any of our times and before phones or social media. What we do not often see or hear is how men do the exact same thing. Now even the bible does not really shine a whole lot of light on men's actions as compared to women. So, I would remind you that women have been second class citizens to some degree for centuries. In fact, women are still fighting this battle today in 2021. Long story short men get caught up in their feelings and emotions. The problem with getting too caught up in our emotions and feelings is that it has all types of consequences that come as a result of it. In fact, men have referenced the scripture text below as the root cause to all our problems even as of today. I don't disagree in totality; however, there are a few additional stones left needing to be overturned. I know some of the readers may be remarkably familiar with the scripture I am getting ready to introduce below but I am not sure if you can unpack the same understanding. Therefore, lets us examine closely what is happening here in this early text of scripture.

Genesis 2:4-3:24 New International Version (NIV)

⁴ This is the account of the heavens and the earth when they were created, when the LORD God made the earth and the heavens.

⁵ Now no shrub had yet appeared on the earth[a] and no plant had yet sprung up, for the LORD God had not sent rain on the earth and there was no one to work the ground, ⁶ but streams[b] came up from the earth and watered the whole surface of the ground. ⁷ Then the LORD God formed a man[c] from the dust of the ground and breathed into his nostrils the breath of life, and the man became a living being.

> **Points to Consider:** We discover here the creation of the world, as believers understand. A total opposite of evolution or what scientist would have us to believe. The world is new and is in need of someone to live and dwell on the earth amongst all creation. God creates Adam. The very first man out of the dust or dirt of the earth in his own image and breathe his very breath into him. Hmm no wonder that when we die, we are buried and returned to the dirt of the earth that we were first created from. More so than that we are created in the image and likeness of God. Wow, this is extremely important to know. How often do you realize this? We are created in the very imagine of God and

he breathe his very own breath into us and we had and have life? Take a second and really think on this powerful statement, it should make you think differently of yourself. The very next time you look in the mirror I want you to remember you are created in the image of God.

⁸ Now the LORD God had planted a garden in the east, in Eden; and there he put the man he had formed. ⁹ The LORD God made all kinds of trees grow out of the ground—trees that were pleasing to the eye and good for food. In the middle of the garden were the tree of life and the tree of the knowledge of good and evil.

Points to Consider: Important information to know, Ellen van Wolfe noted that among Bible scholars "the trees are almost always dealt with separately and not related to each other" and that "attention is almost exclusively directed to the tree of knowledge of good and evil, whereas the tree of life is paid hardly any attention." **Forbidden fruit** is a name given to the **fruit** growing in the Garden of Eden which **God** commands mankind not to eat. In the biblical narrative, Adam and Eve ate the **fruit** from the tree of the knowledge of good and evil and are exiled from Eden. In the Book of Genesis, the tree of life is first described in chapter 2, verse 9 as being "in the midst of the Garden of Eden" with the tree of the knowledge of good and evil (Hebrew). After the fall of man, "lest he put forth his hand, and take also of the tree of life, and eat, and live forever",[2] cherubim are placed at the east end of the Garden to guard the way to the tree of life. Now here is where the saga begins with this scripture in verse 15. We see God giving a command to the man not the woman. This becomes an overly critical part of the story where we see controversy on the horizon. Make a mental note that when God gives this command the woman is not even on the scene, in fact she has not been created. This command was given directly to Adam and not Eve. The directive was noticeably clear or so it would seem at this point. As you continue to read you will see that from this noticeably clear directive there are some extremely specific consequences that will come. In fact, it happens all the time before we caught up. God sends clear warnings; however, we override them because during the time we receive them all is well in our world.

[15] The LORD God took the man and put him in the Garden of Eden to work it and take care of it. [16] And the LORD God commanded the man, "You are free to eat from any tree in the garden; [17] but you must not eat from the tree of the knowledge of good and evil, for when you eat from it you will certainly die." [18] The LORD God said, "It is not good for the man to be alone. I will make a helper suitable for him."

[19] Now the LORD God had formed out of the ground all the wild animals and all the birds in the sky. He brought them to the man to see what he would name them; and whatever the man called each living creature, that was its name. [20] So the man gave names to all the livestock, the birds in the sky and all the wild animals.

But for Adam[f] no suitable helper was found. [21] So the LORD God caused the man to fall into a deep sleep; and while he was sleeping, he took one of the man's ribs[g] and then closed up the place with flesh. [22] Then the LORD God made a woman from the rib[h] he had taken out of the man, and he brought her to the man.

[23] The man said, "This is now bone of my bones and flesh of my flesh; she shall be called 'woman,' for she was taken out of man." [24] That is why a man leaves his father and mother and is united to his wife, and

they become one flesh. [25] Adam and his wife were both naked, and they felt no shame.

> **Points to Consider:** Wow, everyone in the garden is straight up naked, and innocent. All appears to be going well in the world of Adam and Eve. The two of them are living their best life and so are the animals. The animals and everyone in the garden are good and there is not a care in the world just living and letting live. No confusion at all Adam and Eve both are good.

The Fall

3 Now the serpent was craftier than any of the wild animals the LORD God had made. He said to the woman, "Did God really say, 'You must not eat from any tree in the garden'?"

> **Points to Consider:** Wow, I don't know about you, but if none of the other animals are talking and suddenly, the serpent roles up on me talking, hmmm Houston, we have a problem. Right here is where things go wrong fast. The bible does not make mention of any other animals talking or having conversation. I do not know but it seems like this would have stopped Eve in her tracks but it does not. She does not see anything wrong with the serpent talking. So what can we learn from Eve's comfort in talking to the serpent? Perhaps what we learn from this incredibly unique interaction is that talking with the animals was common although there is no mentioning of these interactions as being normal. This would make things a lot simpler if there were some mentioning of the animal's ability to talk. So here we are the serpent now pose a question. I do not believe the question is a difficult question. In fact, it would

appear as if this question should have been a common question that could or should have been answered with extreme ease. What we do discover here is that critical thinking is perhaps important to have. So here we go with the drama. The only thing the serpent does is cause her to think about the directive given to Adam by God and shared with her by Adam. These little details become especially important based on the first and second outcomes of man meaning Adam and Eve's actions. I must admit having education as my profession causes me to wonder how much importance was placed on the sharing from God to Adam and Adam to Eve. There have been times I question how much stress did Adam place on this extremely specific directive. Then I must remind myself that it is Eve who relays this message to the serpent, therefore it would appear that it was self-explanatory death is death. The problem is at this point does Eve really understand what death really means considering that there had never been any death of a human being at this point? Obedience is the key here and the serpent chips away at Eve's confidence in obeying what God has commanded. However I think it is important to ask the question how great of a teacher was Adam. Did Adam check for understanding from Eve? Considering he is the man and he is ultimately accountable to God for the Garden.

[2] The woman said to the serpent, "We may eat fruit from the trees in the garden, [3] but God did say, 'You must not eat fruit from the tree that is in the middle of the garden, and you must not touch it, or you will die.'"

[4] "You will not certainly die," the serpent said to the woman. [5] "For God knows that when you eat from it your eyes will be opened, and you will be like God, knowing good and evil."

⁶ When the woman saw that the fruit of the tree was good for food and pleasing to the eye, and also desirable for gaining wisdom, she took some and ate it. She also gave some to her husband, who was with her, and he ate it. ⁷ Then the eyes of both of them were opened, and they realized they were naked; so they sewed fig leaves together and made coverings for themselves.

Points to Consider:

To me this story becomes progressively worst. The reason I say the story becomes progressively worst is for two reasons.

First reason is that Adam is right there with her, at some point he should have intervened and said that this is ludicrous let us go I have heard enough. I mean why is he listening to this foolishness and allowing it to even go down like this? Adam has a responsibility to Eve especially considering he was given this directive directly from God and passed it down to Eve.

Second reason this story gets progressively worst is because God would come down in the cool of the evening and speak with them both. The serpent comes along out of the blue and the relationship they have with God is blown up just that easy. This example has to make you wonder why it is so easy for someone we hardly know to come in so easy and disrupt our relationship with God. One would think well if God is coming down in the cool of the evening and spending time with man that for this reason alone, the relationship between man and God should be tight and the serpent would not have been able to easily deceive them into eating from the tree. One would have to ask himself was Adam and Eve secretly jealous or envious of God's ability to come and go in and out of the garden or maybe they were overwhelmed by his vast wisdom and knowledge so much so that they were willing to do anything just to be equals?

[8] Then the man and his wife heard the sound of the LORD God as he was walking in the garden in the cool of the day, and they hid from the LORD God among the trees of the garden. [9] But the LORD God called to the man, "Where are you?"

[10] He answered, "I heard you in the garden, and I was afraid because I was naked; so I hid."

[11] And he said, "Who told you that you were naked? Have you eaten from the tree that I commanded you not to eat from?"

[12] The man said, "The woman you put here with me—she gave me some fruit from the tree, and I ate it." [13] Then the LORD God said to the woman, "What is this you have done?"

The woman said, "The serpent deceived me, and I ate."

[14] So the LORD God said to the serpent, "Because you have done this,

"Cursed are you above all livestock
    and all wild animals! You will crawl on your belly and you will eat dust all the days of your life. [15] And I will put enmity between you and the woman,
    and between your offspring[i] and hers;
he will crush[j] your head,
    and you will strike his heel."

[16] To the woman he said,

"I will make your pains in childbearing very severe;
    with painful labor you will give birth to children.
Your desire will be for your husband,
    and he will rule over you."

¹⁷ To Adam he said, "Because you listened to your wife and ate fruit from the tree about which I commanded you, 'You must not eat from it, 'Cursed is the ground because of you;

through painful toil you will eat food from it all the days of your life.
¹⁸ It will produce thorns and thistles for you,

and you will eat the plants of the field.
¹⁹ By the sweat of your brow

you will eat your food
until you return to the ground,

since from it you were taken;
for dust you are

and to dust you will return."

²⁰ Adam[k] named his wife Eve,[l] because she would become the mother of all the living.

²¹ The LORD God made garments of skin for Adam and his wife and clothed them. ²² And the LORD God said, "The man has now become like one of us, knowing good and evil. He must not be allowed to reach out his hand and take also from the tree of life and eat, and live forever." ²³ So the LORD God banished him from the Garden of Eden to work the ground from which he had been taken. ²⁴ After he drove the man out, he placed on the east side[m] of the Garden of Eden cherubim and a flaming sword flashing back and forth to guard the way to the tree of life.

Points to Consider: I am Not mad, I am just in my Feelings Summary

Wow, it is hard to believe, but easy to say what we would have done. This story is better than any soap opera you will ever see. Look at how everyone got so caught up in their feelings and did not want to take responsibility for their actions, instead everyone blames someone else. I am not shocked that Eve blames the serpent and I would not be shocked if Adam blames the serpent as well. What does shock me is how Adam instantly blames God. Wow that blows me away. I still cannot believe that Adam has the nerve now to stand up and blame God for giving him Eve and it is his fault for giving her to him when all along he could have step in at any time and stopped all the nonsense from ever happening. I know you may have never looked at it from this prospective, but it is all going down for real right here in the Garden. The blame game is on for real. Nobody wants to man up and say it was me or I am the reason everything happened the way it happens.

Adam must have really been in his feelings to make such a bold statement at this point. I guess Adam says I am not going to shoulder the responsibility for this one alone. I often wondered if Adam had stepped up and been accountable for his own actions would the outcome have been different. This story has always amazed me because I like how God places emphasis on who told you that you were naked. I can instantly vision God as and angry, upset or plain disappointed about this outcome. I would not dare say that God got in his feelings based on how he responds but, its kind of sounds like he did. No disrespect, but I just feel his disappointment in man in this interaction. Excuse how I preface this culturally from an African American prospective but it is as if I can hear Gods fatherly voice now, who done went told you something I really was not ready to share with you just yet or at this time. Now I am thinking out loud somebody has gone and let the cat out of the bag.

Can you imagine being a child or from a parent's point of view someone tells your child about a topic you had not plan on discussing with them at that appointed time? As a loving father, I can feel through this interaction or exchange God is not pleased because he knows the impact it is going to have on their lives. Like any caring parent you want to protect your children from experiences that they are not quite mature enough to handle at the time. This clearly shows how their innocence has been taken away from them. I mean they were naked before when God would come to the garden to talk and it was all good. One really great example if you have experience it would be, how freely a little kid runs through the house naked doing whatever he or she feels like doing until someone tells them this is inappropriate, and they should not be doing it.

Here we see and hear them say, we are afraid because we are naked, Man I understand God's disappointment in their new discovery before their time. As a parent I would never want someone to expose my child to sex or a conversation about sex before their appropriate time or age. To everything there is a season and a time for it. Think about it they were out there sewing leaves together to hide their private parts whereas before it was not even on the radar. This experience has caused them to be exposed to things God knew that they were not ready for. The consequence of being exposed before the appropriate time has left all of mankind in a pickle to say the least. They were robbed of their innocence's by them on disobedience. The one decision has impacted mankind till this very day. The consequence of Adam and Eve's actions got them tossed out of the Garden that God created for them to live a life of hardship. Tyler Perry could not write a better storyline. I hope this gets you excited about reading your bible. This is only the beginning and there is so much more in store for us to explore and learn together.

Brothers against Brothers

First family drama, is about how two brothers with great intentions sow an offering to God. One brother's offering was well received and the other brother's was not. Based on jealously, one brother, kills the other one. This story for some is awfully familiar. The story is used to show many illustrations and examples. A great example of brotherly love, or the lack thereof. In reading this story throughout the years, I have often wondered how these two brothers offering to the Lord was so uniquely different. I want to first point out that this is the very first family history so there is a lot of unknowns and they did not have any examples to pull from like we do today; so it is always easy to say what you would have done until you find yourself in this situation. Now, let us delve into this story.

Cain and Abel

4 Now Adam knew Eve his wife, and she conceived and bore Cain, saying, "I have gotten[a] a man with the help of the Lord." ² And again, she bore his brother Abel. Now Abel was a keeper of sheep, and Cain a worker of the ground. ³ In the course of time Cain brought to the Lord an offering of the fruit of the ground, ⁴ and Abel also brought of the firstborn of his flock and of their fat portions. And the Lord had regard for Abel and his offering, ⁵ but for Cain and his offering he had no regard. So, Cain was terribly angry, and his face fell. ⁶ The Lord said to Cain, "Why are you angry, and why has your face fallen? ⁷ If you do well, will you not be accepted?[b] And if you do not do well, sin is crouching at the door. Its desire is contrary to[c] you, but you must rule over it."

Points to Consider: This is an enormously powerful point that I pray each reader gains a full understanding of, because this is a teaching moment in the text. In fact, this has been a puzzling matter I have been hoping to resolve for years or at least since I first heard this story. The story has been such a mystery to me, and no one has ever been able to break these points down for me so I contribute my finds to that information that the Holy Spirit has revealed to me and I hope to reveal this to you as the reader. I believe for understanding purpose it is important to understand a few common definitions. For example, the definition regard is of extreme importance! I have always recommended that the purchase of a one-dollar dictionary from the Dollar tree could open up your biblical understanding more or just as much as some of the books you will purchase for fifty to one hundred dollars.

The drama all starts over the very intent of an offering unto the Lord. Seems frivolous from the onset, but it is much deeper than one can see from the naked eye without spiritual insight. I am not sure how many readers have had this same question as to why it was such a big deal to God and to Able for that matter. This senseless murder could have and should have been prevented. In my initial opinion it just seems as if this is not worth being so angry over or killing your brother over.

I strongly believe this information reveals the intentions behind the difference in one brother's offering over the other brother's offering. We clearly see that both gave an offering and for all intense purpose we want to believe the two offerings are almost equal but not so. How can we determine what went wrong, why it went wrong and how does it end up with one brother killing the other brother? The other brother being marked and sent into exile. I believe this information will cause you to look at your giving totally different and from a fresh and renewed prospective. Not as to give solely from the mindset of duty or obligation without a deeper meaning, understanding and purpose. Giving like most things with God begins with a heart matter.

The question one must begin to try to understand is that God understands and discerns man's heart and his inner most thoughts. We see in the New Testament writing reveal through Christ Jesus. The New Testament writing often reference that Jesus discern the heart of men. One of the many the difference in us and God is that we can get so caught up in the mere fact that someone gave us something, rather than the intents or motive behind the why. God looks at the very intent of our heart regarding the matter of giving. Based on humanistic nature we can become distracted by the gifts, without realizing it is a trick of the enemy. The enemy sends us distractions to prevent us from operating in Gods perfect purpose and plan for our lives.

Ask yourself this question. Have you ever just given something because you were required to do give it and you took no pleasure or pride in the importance of giving?

Here is what God says about the two brothers Cain and Able concerning their offerings. One he regards and the other he does not so what does this means? Back to the definition for clarity of though and understanding.

Regard means when you give someone a good, long look, you regard them. Regard_often means respect and admiration, as in "I have the greatest regard for my grandmother. So, we see here God's response to Able's offering compared to that of his brother. Wow this is it, I believe this is the hidden ingredient to utterly understand what happened in this situation here. Look at Gods response to Able's offering God makes it abundantly clear how he felt about his giving. God looked upon his heart and attitude towards his giving.

What does God say about Cain's offering? Why does God reject his offering? Why does Cain become so angry? My goal is to unlock this mystery. To see what God's thoughts here we must seek the understanding of the antonym and synonyms of the word regard. This same conversation reveals Gods take on the word regard for Abel was the Antonym's meaning of the word regard and for Cain it was the Synonym's meaning of the word regard. There is a huge lesson to be learned here in understanding the differences. I do not believe one can even begin to understand the complexity of the why and the how with this contextual information being revealed.

Antonyms for Regard: miss, overlook, disregard, despise, dislike, contemn, hate, loathe,

Synonyms for Regard: behold, view, contemplate, esteem, consider, deem, affect, respect, reverence, revere, value, conceive, heed, notice, mind.

There is an incredibly unique difference in how God sees Abel's offering compared to that of his brother Cain's. This teaches us that we must make sure that when we give our time our resources or whatever we give, it must be with the right heart and motive. This is a wonderful example of how important our giving is to God. Therefore, whenever or whatever we give make sure our heart and motives are right and pure, if not get your heart and motives right before you give. My recommendation is to immediately repent and ask God for forgiveness and give from a grateful heart, that it may be received well. There is nothing wrong with taking some time and refocus our minds and thoughts before we give. This will keep you out of your feeling and from getting mad. This can be obtained if we check ourselves before we get caught up in our emotions.

This is also a leaning opportunity for both Cain and Able to grow from just like for us to grow from, but we get mad at correction and get all caught up in our feelings and why me attitude whenever something happens to us all the time. We must learn to control what we can control and trust God to do the rest. When we decide to do things, our way based on our emotions like what Cain does to his brother, the result is never good. People can do all manner of evil to you and against you or stop speaking to one another. The lack of communication never helps; it only worsens the matter. Communication is critically important when it is matters of the heart. What is most important in cases such as these two brothers is you must seek first to understand and then to be understood with the heart of humility and forgiveness.

Brother Drama Continues

[8] Cain spoke to Abel his brother.[d] And when they were in the field, Cain rose up against his brother Abel and killed him. [9] Then the LORD said to Cain, "Where is Abel your brother?" He said, "I do not know; am I my brother's keeper?" [10] And the LORD said, "What have you done? The voice of your brother's blood is crying to me from the ground. [11] And now you are cursed from the ground, which has opened its mouth to receive your brother's blood from your hand. [12] When you work the ground, it shall no longer yield to you its strength. You shall be a fugitive and a wanderer on the earth." [13] Cain said to the LORD, "My punishment is greater than I can bear.[e] [14] Behold, you have driven me today away from the ground, and from your face I shall be hidden. I shall be a fugitive and a wanderer on the earth, and whoever finds me will kill me." [15] Then the LORD said to him, "Not so! If anyone kills Cain, vengeance shall be taken on him sevenfold." And the LORD put a mark on Cain, lest any who found him should attack him. [16] Then Cain went away from the presence of the LORD and settled in the land of Nod,[f] east of Eden.

Points to Consider: So, what we see here is a total disregard for one's feelings or opinions. Cain already knew in his heart what he had planned to do. This plan was revealed to him by God, along with wisdom from God as to how to move forward. I believe if Cain had only taken a few moments and listened to what God was saying we would be reading this story totally different.

However, just like some of us Cain's anger and disenchantment got the best of him and now he only wants to get even with his brother. An innocent biological bother who meant him no harm, and had not done anything to him. So, do not be naive and think that people including family will not try and harm you. We discover here how God gives warning before destruction. He shares with Cain how he appeared. Given him the opportunity to check his feelings before he acts on them. By asking the questions: why are you angry and why has your face fallen? This was a subtle warning from God to Cain. I can envision God saying to Cain, I see you mad; it is all over your face in plain sight. Cain could have tried to get it together then, especially when God says to Cain if you do well you will be accepted. In so many words or ways he is telling Cain repent and get it right. Cain should have immediately repented and as God if he could resubmit his offering. Then all would be well with the world, Able, and most importantly God. Then God warns him again by telling him if you do not get yourself together sin is right there at your door. God shares with him the power of sin, either you rule over it or it rules over you. Like a loving father God gives Cain wise counsel.

So, Cain was very angry, and his face fell. We can clearly see that Cain is caught up into his feelings. Cain doesn't appear to have the capacity to understand the wise counsel from God. [6] The LORD said to Cain, "Why are you angry, and why has your face fallen? [7] If you do well, will you not be accepted?[b] And if you do not do well, sin is crouching at the door. Its desire is contrary to[c] you, but you must rule over it."

CHAPTER 3

ENTANGLEMENT (INSECURITIES IN THE MARRIAGE)

[110] Now there was a famine in the land. So, Abram went down to Egypt to sojourn there, for the famine was severe in the land. [11] When he was about to enter Egypt, he said to Sarai his wife, "I know that you are a woman beautiful in appearance, [12] and when the Egyptians see you, they will say, 'This is his wife.' Then they will kill me, but they will let you live. [13] Say you are my sister, that it may go well with me because of you, and that my life may be spared for your sake."

Points to Consider: Here is another amazing story about two high profile people in the bible. One could look at their marriage and say if it was not for having a baby later in life the marriage was exemplary. We do not see their beginnings, but we see them later in their lives and marriage. We see them as a married couple who develop a relationship with God with little to no worries.

Like the two of them we must learn to nurture our relationship with God as this allows us to become who God has created for us to be. Like us these two have a life filled with obstacles and situations where they keep getting themselves into trouble. This should sound familiar to all of us especially married couples. The divorce rate is at an all-time high. A big part of that is simply because we cannot agree. Here we see that the two of them agree, but this agreement is created out of fear and low self-esteem issues.

Let me begin by saying I knew Sarai was beautiful, but man I had no idea her beauty was on this kind of level. I mean when your wife is this beautiful you are bound to get into some trouble as the husband of a wife of such beauty.

So here we see Abram and Sarai before their names are changed by God and they are headed to Egypt because of hunger. This journey lands them into chaos and drama. Here we have Abram afraid and insecure because of his wife's beauty. This lets us know that Sarai had to be a fine and pretty young thing. I mean she is so beautiful where Abram is afraid to call her his own wife because he fears he will be put to death because of her beauty. Wow, that is rough to be married to someone that beautiful. So, Abram has come up with a plan out of fear to save his life because his wife is so beautiful.

Maybe it is just me but I am thinking yes, his life is in jeopardy possibly, but what is going to happen to Sarai. Is her life not going to be in equal jeopardy once they find out she is single and ready to mingle? I am thinking since she does not belong to a man then every loose dog is now going to be sniffing around trying to get her. To me this does not sound like a good plan but possibly Abram has run into this problem before because he comes up with this lie way to easy. Sounds to me like this happened before and possibly worked if not the risk is just too risky.

[14] When Abram entered Egypt, the Egyptians saw that the woman was very beautiful. [15] And when the princes of Pharaoh saw her, they praised her to Pharaoh. And the woman was taken into Pharaoh's house. [16] And for her sake he dealt well with Abram; and he had sheep, oxen, male donkeys, male servants, female servants, female donkeys, and camels.

Points to Consider: How often have you seen someone that is so beautiful that you can agree with someone else and then run tell of the beauty of the individual you just saw. So, we see something here that we do not normally see in the bible and that is the level of someone's beauty. I mean I am not sure how often the bible speaks of a woman's beauty but here we have someone so beautiful that they ran back and told the king. Now mind you, you do not just come tell the king about some average beautiful woman, her beauty had to be beyond compare.

Wow, did you know that Sarai was this beautiful? You know you are beautiful when other beautiful women run and talk about you. Looks like Abram was on to something that is why I said he had to have had this experience before. To say he had run into this problem before is easy to assume because he intuitively knew that he had better not tell the truth about his own wife or else face severe consequences. Abram knew he was about to get caught up all because of Sara, his beautiful wife. The problem here is, you would think he should or would instantly consult with God, but he does the exact opposite; he went and decided without speaking with God concerning the matter.

This makes me wonder what is going on with Abram, perhaps he was like some of us can be. He possibly said to himself God does not have time to deal with these lowly matters concerning us, so I better handle this one on my own. Does that sound familiar to you? We have all been in a place where we try to handle things on our own only to have to come back and eventually leave it all at the altar with God. I cannot even begin to count the number of times I tried to resolve matters on my own, thinking I knew what was best, only to mess everything and everyone around me up in the end. Think about it, the reason he goes to Egypt is because there is a famine in the land. Is it just me or should he have asked God for provision since it was God's vision, he was attempting to carry out? Surely God would make provision for his vision if he asked him. Here we see Abram just as we see ourselves not willing to ask God for help and about to make a royal mess of our lives. This happens all the time especially those of us who are the children of God. The reason I say this is because we get so caught up in ourselves that we sometimes forget the powerful God that we serve. A classic example of getting caught up in our feelings. Let us see what happens next, I am excited what about you?

[17] But the LORD afflicted Pharaoh and his house with great plagues because of Sarai, Abram's wife. [18] So Pharaoh called Abram and said, "What is this you have done to me? Why did you not tell me that she was your wife? [19] Why did you say, 'She is my sister,' so that I took her for my wife? Now then, here is your wife; take her, and go." [20] And Pharaoh gave men orders concerning him, and they sent him away with his wife and all that he had.

Points to Consider: Oh my, look at this right here. God is always looking out for us even when we are not looking out for ourselves. We see that because of this lie that Abram has convinced his wife Sarai to go along with what has been exposed. And look who exposed this diabolical lie to Pharaoh, none other but God. The funny thing is its no man or woman who snitched on Abram it was God who expose the lie to Pharaoh. I do not know about you, but to me this is so hilarious however, it shows how someone else's life can affect your entire household. Abram lied and as a result, his lies affected Pharaoh's entire household.

We see here Pharaoh's House was filled with plagues. The interesting thing I discovered here is that we see Pharaoh some centuries prior to Moses whose house suffers from plagues like that of the Pharaoh during the time of Abram's decedents being captives in slavery. This is so ironic for the readers who understand the story or perhaps are biblical scholars. I was not aware that this had taken place years before God use Moses to bring plagues to Egypt.

Wow, so Pharaoh is Big mad at Abram and rightfully so. Pharaoh should be mad at Abram for telling him this lie and getting his house filled with plagues. All because he refuses to be honest and just tell the truth about his wife. Pharaoh confronts Abram and said why you did not tell me she was your wife rather than your sister? I would imagine that Abram was so afraid of what would happen to him he just did not know what to do. Abram temporally lost his mind and just told what he thought was a little white lie just to get through. I know it is extremely easy to point the finger at him and say why in the world would he tell this lie when the truth would do. This is more reason why he should have consulted with God First. Abram has now allowed himself and Sarai his wife to go through some very unnecessary drama all for nothing or at least in the reader's eyes who is reading about this event that is happening and is happening to him and his wife all due to a lie he felt like he just had to tell.

This lie has such a huge impact on everyone involved with it. One would think that Abram would never let the lie go this far. The reason this is so awful is because we see here that Abram allowed this lie to go so far that Pharaoh and Sarai perform an actual marriage ceremony and all the trimmings that come along with doing a wedding ceremony. In fact, according to the scriptures he had already taken her as his wife. The plot has gotten so thick that maybe Abram felt even more pressure to keep the lie going now. I am thinking he felt extremely helpless and did not know what to do. Think about how big this one lie has developed into.

My question is if you love your wife why allow this to go on any further and especially not allow them to get married without stepping up and admitting to his lying. So, you like drama, well here it is, at its absolute best, all in the bible. Man, this is better than any soap opera. How could Abram carry the lie so far, I mean if God does not come in and cause these plagues to happen how in the world does he plan to get Sarai out of the house of Pharaoh? Wow this is better than reality T.V.

show or Lifetime movie. Who would think that this would happen to Abram the man of God the father of all fathers?

Pharaoh is furious and he is so mad that he says here is your wife take her and go. He is not thinking of her beauty at this point because he is pissed off to the highest level. He goes so far to give orders for him and his wife and all his belongings to go. Man, he is mad and again rightfully so. Here he is thinking he has scored him a brand-new beautiful bride only to end up with a house filled with plagues. Pharaoh got rid of her, Abram and the whole house immediately. This reminds me again of the years to come when Pharaoh again must let God's people go without a scrap or scratch. This is powerful! God had to be with Abram because I am certain this treasonous action called for death to Abram. I think I would have had to do something to Abram and Sarai, but we see here that he does nothing. I am confident it is out of the fear and admiration of God. Look at God's powerful reach. I am not sure about you, but this information was all new to me until I studied and researched it. I am better as a result of knowing that this lie created out of fear and may have caused Abram and Sarai their lives, if God had not stepped in. This is a wonderful example of how God continues to pull us out of dangerous decisions we make for ourselves. The scripture does not say that Abram cried out before the Lord or petition God for help in this situation. What we see here is Sarai has been taken as Pharaoh's Wife. There are lots of unknown variables here, for example had he slept with her and as a result these plagues happen why are we at this point where we see he has already taken her as his wife. Interestingly, the moral of the story from this prospective is God comes in and rescues us when we create dilemmas for ourselves. What a tangled web that they had weaved that God stepped in to untangle them. This is not the last of this couple because the plot thickens.

The Original Baby Moma Drama #1 Sarai and Hagar

Currently, we see so much that goes on with families and children happening today. For instance, we see baby mama drama all the time. I mean you can turn the television on and see it daily on the Maury Pavlovich show with titles like "Who Is the Baby's Daddy". Well, I bet a lot of readers thought that this just started happening in the twenty centuries but not so. This problem has been going on for ages and ages. What's interesting is that this originally started back with Sarai and Hagar. The drama is no less theatrical than your everyday drama on shows on T.V today. So, let us take a close look into the lives of these two women and the drama that birth two nations as a result of it all. This story is very complexed to say the least. We have God's main servant Abram, his wife Sarai and their Egyptian servant as the main characters. All the drama is circulated around a married couple who was promised by God to have a son and God was not moving fast enough according to their plans. Sarai comes up with a great idea as to how to speed up the process by throwing in a baby and we have some baby mama issues and everyone is in their feelings. We discover yet again a group of people trying to step up and be God or at least help God with his promises. The unfortunate thing about learning of God's plan for your life is, we become impatient with the manifestation of the promises. Humanistically, we do not often have the wherewithal to handle knowing this information without becoming impatient with the process. Here we see a husband and wife given a promise by God that has yet to come to pass. The wife comes up with what she believes as a great idea or strategy as to how to expedite God's plan. The plan backfires and there is a lot of finger pointing and chaos. God intervenes. Let us take a didactic look at these next scriptures.

16 Now Sarai, Abram's wife, had borne him no children. She had a female Egyptian servant whose name was Hagar. ² And Sarai said to Abram, "Behold now, the LORD has prevented me from bearing children. Go in unto my servant; it may be that I shall obtain children[1] by her." And Abram listened to the voice of Sarai. [3] So, after Abram [c]had lived ten years in the land of Canaan, Sarai, Abram's wife, took Hagar the Egyptian, her servant, and gave her to Abram her husband as a wife. [4] And he went in to Hagar, and she conceived. And when she saw that she had conceived, she looked with contempt on her mistress.[2] [5] And Sarai said to Abram, "May the wrong done to me be on you! I gave my servant to your embrace, and when she saw that she had conceived, she looked on me with contempt. May [g]the LORD judge between you and me!" [6] But Abram said to Sarai, "Behold, your servant is in your power; do to her as you please." Then Sarai dealt harshly with her, and she fled from her.

Points to Consider: Here we see Sarai, Abram's wife has yet to bare him a child and it appears she is a bit perturb with God not moving according to her timeline with having a baby. The reason she appears perturb is because she states to her husband Abram that God has prevented her from bearing any children. This is classic finger pointing. So, Sarai comes up with this great idea of having her husband Abram go in and sleep with her Egyptian servant that she may bear children for her. Now the plot has thickened; who in their right mind allows this to happen? In Sarai's defense she is not of childbearing age and there have been years between God's promise and her current statues. So, in Sarai mind she figures I can still have what I want and desire through my servant. Does this sound like a bad idea? Think about it she should not have to go through the morning sickness or the pain of delivery and still get the same results. I believe in her mind she sees this as a win-win situation. However, it is just not that simple because there is so much more to this than what meets the eye. Sarai did not count on some of the internal feelings that she would have to deal with from allowing the servant to birth a child for her husband, something she was unable to do herself.

I find it remarkably interesting that Abram has no problem with this request and he agrees to go along with it. There is no record that he objected to this request at all. So, I have always wondered what his thinking was since he was the one who had the greater relationship with God at this point. Abram was the one declared to be the father of many nations. In acknowledging this information one who think that Abram would not listen to Sarai his wife and instead remind her that God is faithful to his word and he would deliver his promise. We do not see that Abram listened to Sarai but instead married his wife's servant and she bared him a child. Things seem to be going well or at least we see that her plan has manifested. The problem comes in where Sarai starts to feel like now Hagar is looking at her like she better than her because she's been able to do something for Abram that Sarai has yet to be able to do so Sarai starts to feel some type of way. I would like to explain her emotions as hurt, bitter, and jealous. These internal emotions caused her to have some issues with the plot that she herself put into action. Sarai did not intend for her servant to become high minded after becoming pregnant by Abram. Sarah being the first wife probably felt that Hagar needed to remain in her place as a servant. The interesting about this is Hagar was no longer a servant because she was given to Abram by Sarai as a wife. I would think that with this being considered how then does Sarai have the audacity to blame Abram or be mad at Hagar because she started feeling empowered as the women who bore Abram his first son.

This caused Sarai to confront Abram to the point he threw his hands up and said she is your servant do what you want with her. This statement cause Sarai to deal harshly with Hagar to the point that she fled. The bible does give the details, but I can't imagine that Sarai really turned the heat up on her and caused her to double her work load, and interfered with any sense of comfort, stability or power that Hagar received as being Abram's wife. In short Sarai made her life a living hell, to the point she said enough is enough and fled. God must intervene, provide structure, encouragement and hope.

[7] The angel of the LORD found her by a spring of water in the wilderness, the spring on the way to *f*Shur. [8] And he said, "Hagar, servant of Sarai, where have you come from and where are you going?" She said, "I am fleeing from my mistress Sarai." [9] The angel of the LORD said to her, "Return to your mistress and submit to her." [10] The angel of the LORD also said to her, *g*"I will surely multiply your offspring so that they cannot be numbered for multitude." [11] And the angel of the LORD said to her,

"Behold, you are pregnant
    and shall bear a son.
You shall call his name Ishmael,*2*
    because the LORD has listened to your affliction.
[12] He shall be *i*a wild donkey of a man,
    his hand against everyone
    and everyone's hand against him,
and he shall dwell over against all his kinsmen."

[13] So she called the name of the LORD who spoke to her, "You are a God of seeing,"*3* for she said, truly here I have seen him who looks after me."*5* [14] Therefore the well was called *l*Beer-lahai-roi;*6* it lies between Kadesh and Bered.

[15] And Hagar bore Abram a son, and Abram called the name of his son, whom Hagar bore, Ishmael. [16] Abram was eighty-six years old when Hagar bore Ishmael to Abram.

Points to Consider: Wow, we see God intervene here and provide wise counsel to Hagar. He tells her to go back and submit to your mistress. In other words, humble yourself go back under Abram and Sarai roof and know your place. I am sure that was not an easy pill to swallow but the story does end there. He confirms that you are truly pregnant, and you will bear a son and your offspring or family will be so large as a result of the son you are currently carry to the point that they cannot be numbered. This news had to be exciting and motivating to her destiny and the destiny of her son. Initially it appears that Hagar gets the short end of the stick because she is just a servant given away for marriage by her mistress. She has no real future other than to be a slave. We see now that she is blessed and highly favored of the Lord. I say this because when she ran God did not have to intervene. Hagar had a plan and destination worth running to in her mind. This lets me know it was not just a spare of the moment decision but rather well thought out. This is clear when the angel of the Lord asks her where you are coming from and where are you going; she was able to clearly express where she was going without hesitation. She was not easily found because it said the angel of the lord had to look for her and found her. What this says to me is that she was fed up and determined to get away. I can only image her frustration and rationale for leaving. This bold decision to run away from her situation caused her to discover some awesome news about her future and the future of her family. I would have asked some additional questions about the description about the child she was carrying. For example, he is describing to be a wild donkey of a man and all sorts of people will be against him. Perhaps she is just so excited to hear some good news that she did not want to go into details about the statements about her son. I mean to have confirmation that she was carrying a male child alone probably consumed her thoughts. I would imagine she tuned the rest out. I want to warn each reader to remember we are reading as learned people, and she was not learned or had the ability to read about these things or different likes we are doing here today with her life or the life of Abram and Sara. The other thing I would ask that you bear in mind that God has not changed their names at this point so there is yet so much more in stored for them all. This entanglement was quite interesting. Keep reading and leaning.

The impossible becomes possible

We often read and hear about, the wonderful works of God therefore to intently study his Holy word will increase our faith. When our faith increases there is an open window to the impossible things to become possible in our lives. Faith being the substance of things hoped for the evidence of things not seen. Through these last few encounters, we see the challenges of Abram and Sarai and how their growth has become obvious. The last we discussed was how Sarai and Abram was convinced that their way was the best way. The two of them make a complete mess of things and put a huge strain on their marriage and potentially jeopardized the plans that God had for their lives.

This proves that we do not always know what is best for ourselves and it is important to have an in-depth understanding of the importance of having an ongoing relationship with God. What God promises he will deliver? God is not a man that he should lie nor is he the son of man that he must repent. Trusting God has proven to be the best decision the couple has made. This decision has allowed the promise of God to be manifested in their lives. A lesson that hopefully every reader will receive as well.

We discover in this next set of scriptures that there has been an increase in Abram and Sarai relationship with God. Abram goes from Abram to Abraham and Sarai to Sarah. The increase is made obvious based on Gods decision to change both of their names. The name alone speaks increase on top of that he clearly stated that he was going to bless them. In this next set of scriptures, we see that what man thought was impossible becomes possible through God. God does not just bless them with a son, but he builds a nation through them and this is so much more than just being blessed with a child. God does this during an age and time in their life where they are somewhat hopeless, powerless, and visionless to even perceive the possibilities of a child. Abraham being one hundred years old and Sarah being ninety years old the very concept was so far removed from both of their thoughts but look at God.

Isaac's Birth Promised

[15] And God said to Abraham, "As for Sarai your wife, you shall not call her name Sarai, but Sarah*d* shall be her name. [16] I will bless her, and moreover, I will *c*give*d* you a son by her. I will bless her, and she shall become nations; kings of peoples shall come from her." [17] Then Abraham fell on his face *f*and laughed and said to himself, "Shall a child be born to a man who is a hundred years old? Shall Sarah, who is ninety years old, bear a child?" [18] And Abraham said to God, "Oh that Ishmael might live before you!" [19] God said, "No, but Sarah your wife shall bear you a son, and you shall call his name *h*Isaac.*g* I will establish my covenant with him as an everlasting covenant for his offspring after him. [20] As for Ishmael, I have heard you; behold, I have blessed him and will make him fruitful and multiply him greatly. He shall father twelve princes, and *k*I will make him into a great nation. [21] But *l*I will establish my covenant with Isaac, whom Sarah shall bear to you at this time next year."

Points to Consider: God demonstrates his love for both Abraham and Sarah by providing details of what he would do in their lives. The two of them have been through a lot together and God has been right there every step of the way guiding them and protecting them even when they endangered themselves and even try to act on Gods behalf. Although it was Sarah who attempted to bring forth a child through her

---

servant rather stand on the promise God had made them. God comes through and bless her among women to allow nations and kings to come from her despite her unbelief that God would do it. God also proves to Abraham that his covenant would not be through Ishmael but through the son Sarah would birth. God then tells him that through Isaac I will establish an everlasting covenant for his offspring after him. God is saying here that through Jacob I will establish the even the greater. Most bible scholars recognize that it was through Jacob whose name was also changed to Israel would have twelve sons also known as the twelve tribes of Israel. Little did I know that God also heard Abrahams heart about his son Ishmael. Although Abraham has not mention anything for Ishmael God blesses him based on Abraham's heart and desire. God says, I have heard you; behold, I have blessed him and will make him fruitful and multiply him greatly. He shall father twelve princes, and I will make him into a great nation. This is a big difference from what we heard in the beginning where he is compared to a wild donkey. One especially important revelation to me was the similarity to Jacob. I was not aware of the twelve princes that were birth through him like that of Jacob. This gives even more evidence to the seed of Abraham and the reach that God has extended through Abrahams seed.

God also clarifies to Abram that I will establish my covenant with Isaac, whom Sarah shall bear to you at this time next year. We see God cleaning up any confusion or misconception right here. God says I am going to make a great nation out of Ishmael, but my everlasting covenant shall come through Sarah. I am so grateful and thankful that Sarah has been his ride or die chick she has been by his side through the thick and thin and I must say I am so thankful that she was included with this great prophecy. I mean Sarah deserve to be included because she has been by Abraham's side through all the lies and fake marriages from arranged births to dealing with all the baby momma drama with Hagar.

The benefits of having a relationship with God

Relationships are critical to our success in life. The sooner we fully understand this concept we can work towards having healthy relationships with everyone we are in contact with. I chose to say everyone you meet because we learn through God's word that we are to love our neighbors as we love ourselves. I also discovered that your neighbor is anyone and everyone you meet. These facts take building relationships on a new level and to a level where one would or could see this as an impossible task. Is there anything too hard for God? No there is not, so we must trust God's word and believe on faith to build relationships with mankind.

Can you imagine denying yourself the basic needs in life like air, food, and love? These are the simple needs in life that we can take for granted when asked to give to someone else; however, we expect them from others. Personally when I ask someone for forgiveness, I expect it immediately. On the other hand what is expected of me and some of you is a long process of deliberation. I often want you to do something immediately, but I want to have the opportunity to take my time doing the same thing. This way of thinking is completely unfair and unreasonable. Loving oneself as you love others should cause immediate self evaluation. This concept is all enclusive according to the word of God.

There are some relationships that do take a bit more time and energy to establish clear communication. Our relationship with God is one that has enormous benefits that will save our lives from drama, chaos and even death. (1) Relationships take a lot of work. Relationships take a lot work. (2) Relationships take a lot of work..(3) Relationships take a lot of work especially during those times you do not necessarily want to be bothered or engaged during the time a friend shows up. Friends just popping up at times when you are not prepared to entertain them can be

---

frustrating and unless you absolutely love them, and you are genuinely interested in seeing them be successful or happy in life.

18 And the LORD appeared to him by the [o]oaks[1] of Mamre, as he sat
at the door of his tent in the heat of the day. 2 He lifted up his eyes and
looked, and behold, three men were standing in front of him. [p]When he
saw them, he ran from the tent door to meet them and bowed himself
to the earth 3 and said, "O Lord,[2] if I have found favor in your sight, do
not pass by your servant. 4 Let a [q]little water be brought, and wash your
feet, and rest yourselves under the tree, 5 while I bring a morsel of bread,
that [r]you may refresh yourselves, and after that you may pass on—[s]since
you have come to your servant." So, they said, "Do as you have said."
6 And Abraham went quickly into the tent to Sarah and said, "Quick!
Three seahs[3] of fine flour! Knead it and make cakes." 7 And Abraham
ran to the herd and took a calf, tender and good, and gave it to a young
man, who prepared it quickly. 8 Then he took curds and milk and the
calf that he had prepared, and set it before them. And he stood by them
under the tree while they ate.

Points to Consider: This part has always left me wondering just how did Abraham know that this was God? One would have to imagine that Abraham as the leader was always looking and watching for strangers or danger around his camp where his precious family lived. Another interesting thing it notes is that it was during the heat of the day when your focus is often more given to your circumstances of the heat rather than focusing on the safety and wellbeing of your post. We see here that he immediate recognizes God. The bible does not give any real detail, but God's presence was immensely powerful to someone he has been in relationship with over the years. Think about its God had recused him on various occasions. Abraham would have been incredibly grateful to God and would have developed a very keen sense of God's presence. The scripture details that he rushes to show his desire to make him and his guest feel welcome and ensure that their personal needs where met without request. One of the first things that come to mind is my sheep know my voice and another they will not follow. We see here Abraham knew God's presence and responded according as someone who really desired to meet his needs. He literally begs God to stay and let him cater to his needs but only if he had found favor in God's sight. How often do we respond to God's presence in this manner? Let me be the first to say this is an appropriate response to God's presence. Why would you beg God to stay? This is a God that has rescued him on many occasions and the same God that has led him to his greatest success in life when he was not sure of himself or his destiny. God was the one who found him, provided instruction for him and protected him during his greatest needs and times of adversity. Like Abraham we all should immediately respond to God in a similar manner. God inhabits the praises of his people. When God's presence is manifested we should immediately be grateful and minister unto God. Ministering unto God with our praise and worship for the marvelous things that he has done just like Abraham is doing here. This is not the time to get in our feelings and become selfish. There are times in the past when we were not mature enough to minister to God's needs rather all we wanted is God to minister to our needs, wants and desire. We were not concerned with what God needed or desired instead it was all about us and what needed and desired. I would be willing to go out on a limb and say most church goers around the world go to church based on their need to be ministered to more so than their need to minister to God. Wisdom and maturity in God will tell you that if you minister to God, he is going to automatically minister unto you and your needs. This is a perfect example of Christian Maturity in this story we are reading right now.

One more interesting fact to point out here is we see that there are three men present with God. Could this be God the father, Jesus the son of God, and the Holy Spirit of God visiting Abraham? Please also note that when Abraham asks, they all spoke in agreement. This is only a theory. The scripture gives that fact for us to see. Hmmm, why do the scriptures point out this fact. I think it is unequivocally clear if not why make mention that there are three men and then make it noticeably clear that the voice was God without giving clear indication that it was God who responsed? Important Note: The scripture does not give clear indication of who the three men represented are. It only states one voice spoke and that was the voice of God. Instead, the scriptures reveal there is only one voice speaking here. God often uses his angels to deliver messages and he will provide their names for example, Gabriel and Steven. Three men, one voice makes it quite clear to me. This is a phenomenal discovery here and I am baffled that I never recognized this before. I am so excited for this discovery and I hope each reader is as well. Let us keep plugging along learning more and more about God. There is so much more to discover based on God's willingness to reveal our purpose to those who love him with our whole hearts. If this does not convince you that God is real and the importance of serving him with our whole hearts, I am not sure if anything will.

[9] They said to him, "Where is Sarah your wife?" And he said, "She is [t]in the tent." [10] The LORD said, "I will surely return to you [u]about this time next year, and [v]Sarah your wife shall have a son." And Sarah was listening at the tent door behind him. [11] Now [w]Abraham and Sarah were old, advanced in years. The way of women had ceased to be with Sarah. [12] [x]So Sarah laughed to herself, saying, [y]"After I am worn out, and [z]my lord is old, shall I have pleasure?" [13] The LORD said to Abraham, "Why did Sarah laugh and say, 'Shall I indeed bear a child, now that I am old?' [14] [a]Is anything too hard[d] for the LORD? [b]At the appointed time I will return to you, about this time next year, and Sarah shall have a son." [15] But Sarah denied it,[c] saying, "I did not laugh," for she was afraid. He said, "No, but you did laugh."

Points to Consider: Based on Abraham's desire to please God and minister to God. God again confirms his promise to Abraham and Sarah about the birth of their son. One may ask why now would God mention this. Think from this prospective how often does your faith get weak and you forget about the promises of God when life kicks in. We often must battle the thoughts that come to our minds that are contrary to the promises of God. This is a skill every Christian must develop. The scriptures teach us to let this mind be in me that is also in Christ Jesus. This sounds easy but it is not. I have found myself having to remind me of this sometimes a thousand times throughout the day. The reason for this is because my mind and thoughts are not always pure and of good thoughts. I can find myself often thinking about several things that do not have anything to do with God or God's vision for my life. In simple terms, my thinking can be quite stinky.

We see here God wants to know where your wife Sarah is. Please note that when God ask you a question, he already knows the answer even if you do not. Abraham thought that she was in the tent behind him and that is what he shares with God. What we discover is that Sarah like most of us is somewhere close by listening in on the conversation that Abraham is having with God. God already knows this but rather than point it out he shares with Abraham important news about her and their future all the while knowing that Sarah is near by listening in closely to their entire conversation. While listening to their conversation the scriptures teach us that Sarah laughs to herself not out loud for anyone to hear. In addition, she said to herself why is this happening now that I am worn out and my lord is old. I can imagine her disbelief to the point that she laughs in disbelief of the very possibility she also mentions now that I am old and worn out shall I find pleasure. Sarah's thinking is very typical of men and women now. I think it is quite interesting that she mentions that she is worn out and does not believe that she is capable of having pleasure in this manner. Sarah is utterly shocked and confused with what God has shared. These are some valid questions and reasons to be very honest. This is a clear indication that Sarah's faith had grown weak and God is here to restore her faith in his promises. Interesting point is why does God asks Abraham why Sarah laughed when he does not even know that she is listening in on the conversation. This could be because Abraham was held accountable to keep Sarah and the household encouraged and focused on the promises of God. Sarah denies her laughing or her thoughts of disbelief. Sarah does not recognize that God is all knowing and he has the ability to discern our thoughts. Out of fear she remains faithful to her lie about her not laughing. God does not let that ride easy and he reminds her by saying but you did laugh. I thought it was interesting how God calls her out publicly on her lie. I don't remember or recall God doing anything like this before. God's confronting her on her actions, the level of love and concern for his people and their actions. An overly critical take from this is God not only confirms his promises but reveals them clearly. Is there anything too hard for God? Something we should always remember. There is nothing too hard for God.

CHAPTER 4

SOMETIMES FAMILY CANNOT GO WITH YOU

As we enter this next set of scriptures, we see just how important a strong relationship with God really pays off. The next conversation Abraham has the privilege of being involved in is based on God's future plans and respect that he has developed for Abraham. God decides to let Abraham in on his intentions. God does not have to let us in on his plans or intentions for our lives or our family's lives. The relationship pays off for Abraham because God allows Abraham to not only know what his plans are, but he allows Abraham the opportunity to have a voice on his decision. This is a critical point being made here. God allows Abraham an inside view of his intentions with the opportunity to lobby for his nephew Lot and Lot's family to be spared. There is some convincing to the point God agrees to Abraham's terms. The interesting thing is God initially told Abraham to leave his family and through his disobedience he brings his nephew Lot along. Now we see Lot and his entire family in need of being saved from destruction. Abraham immediately jumps into action to try and save his nephew Lot and his family. The conversation never happens without having a strong relationship with God.

⁶ Then the men set out from there, and they looked down toward Sodom. And Abraham went with them to set them on their way. ¹⁷ The LORD said, ᶜ"Shall I hide from Abraham what I am about to do, ¹⁸ seeing that Abraham shall surely become a great and mighty nation, and all the

nations of the earth shall be *d*blessed in him? [19] For I have *e*chosen*e* him, that he may command his children and his household after him to keep the way of the LORD by doing righteousness and justice, so that the LORD may bring to Abraham what he has promised him." [20] Then the LORD said, "Because *f*the outcry against Sodom and Gomorrah is great and their sin is very grave, [21] *g*I will go down to see whether they have done altogether*z* according to the outcry that has come to me. And if not, *h*I will know."

Points to Consider: I find it extremely interesting that God takes the time to reaffirm the prayers that came before him from the people. The bible does say if the prayers were from the people in the city or around the city. We do know is God has and will always come and see about his people. This proves to me how important we are to God, in case you ever wondered if God really cares. This example proves his great love for us. This demonstration of love is a critical point to know. The reason being is because we will experience times in our life were we don't feel like God knows the hurt and pain we are experiencing. Trust God knows, and he cares about every part of our lives. We see God take an additional step to confirm and reaffirm the prayers of the people about Sodom and Gomorrah. Let's see what he discovers about the going on of this Sodom and Gomorrah.

Abraham Intercedes for Sodom

Points to Consider: God hears our cries even when we do not believe it to be true. We see hear God comes to see about his people based on their cry out against Sodom. God shows himself as a just and fair God through this demonstration. God could have easily just not revealed to Abraham his intentions. I believe God was compelled to do so based on Abrahams response to God showing up unannounced and desperately willing to meet his need out of a pure heart and love for him. Through my studies I do not recall there ever being a time that God allowed someone to be this involved and have direct input and influence on the outcome of another person's life. The conversation Abraham is allowed to have proves God's Love of mankind. The love Abraham has for God pays off big for the entire family for generations to come. Let us read.

²² ⁱSo the men turned from there and went toward Sodom, but Abraham ʲstill stood before the LORD. ²³ Then Abraham drew near and said, ᵏ"Will you indeed sweep away the righteous with the wicked? ²⁴ Suppose there are fifty righteous within the city. Will you then sweep away the place and not spare it for the fifty righteous who are in it? ²⁵ Far be it from you to do such a thing, to put the righteous to death with the wicked, ˡso that the righteous fare as the wicked! Far be that from you! ᵐShall not the Judge of all the earth do what is just?" ²⁶ And the LORD said, ⁿ"If I find at Sodom fifty righteous in the city, I will spare the whole place for their sake."

²⁷ Abraham answered and said, ᵒ"Behold, I have undertaken to speak to the Lord, I who am but dust and ashes. ²⁸ Suppose five of the fifty righteous are lacking. Will you destroy the whole city for lack of five?" And he said, "I will not destroy it if I find forty-five there." ²⁹ Again he spoke to him and said, "Suppose forty are found there." He answered, "For the sake of forty I will not do it." ³⁰ Then he said, "Oh let not the Lord be angry, and I will speak. Suppose thirty are found there." He answered, "I will not do it, if I find thirty there." ³¹ He said, "Behold, I have undertaken to speak to the Lord. Suppose twenty are found there." He answered, "For the sake of twenty I will not destroy it." ³² Then he said, ᵖ"Oh let not the Lord be angry, and I will speak again but this once. Suppose ten are found there." He answered, "For the sake of ten I will not destroy it." ³³ And the LORD went his way, when he had finished speaking to Abraham, and Abraham returned to his place.

Points to Consider: Wow what an intense conversation going on in this conversation with God but Abraham is shown great favor by God.

This chapter discuss how there are times that you want family to go along for the ride with you but it is just not beneficial. This next account of Abraham's life we see that his relationship with God continues to be strengthened. When our relationship with God increases there are all types of benefits that comes our way. We see here that God continues to guide and direct Abraham's steps along the way. God does not force himself on us as to make us follow his counsel he allows us a chance to choose to do so or not. Once we recognize that his counsel comes from an all knowing prospective and he knows the beginning and the end of a situation we begin to listen more carefully and choose to take it in and learn. The problem comes in where we often want to do things our way because it is what makes sense to us. The ongoing problem with this is we can only see from a small lens. The lenses that we are looking through do not have the capacity of knowing the beginning and the end of all things. I know this sounds much easier than it actually is. I mean think about it we like listening to our own advice about a matter rather to seek wise counsel through the word of God and the Holy Spirit or the leaders that God have placed in our lives. There are also times that we pick and choose what parts of God's word or counsel that we are going to use.

In this next set of events, we see what is about to go down could have been prevented if Abraham had listened early on in his walk with God. God clearly ask him to get from among his family. Abraham did just that however he decided to take one of his family members with him. The member he took was his nephew Lot. This does not appear to be a big issue in the beginning. One would even say well it is just his nephew, why not, why is God being so harsh on poor Abraham. Remember God knows the beginning and the end of a matter unlike us. When we listen to God we win but when we choose to listen to only part of his direction and not all we are placing our lives and others lives at risk. Let us see what the scriptures reveals to us next.

God Rescues Lot

19 The ªtwo angels came to Sodom in the evening, and Lot was sitting in the gate of Sodom. When Lot saw them, he rose to meet them and bowed himself with his face to the earth ² and said, "My lords, ʳplease turn aside to your servant's house and spend the night ˢand wash your feet. Then you may rise up early and go on your way." They said, ᵗ"No; we will spend the night in the town square." ³ But he pressed them strongly; so, they turned aside to him and entered his house. And he made them a feast and baked unleavened bread, and they ate.

    Points to Consider: We see hear that Lot recognized the two angels right away. This lets me know that he had to have learned how to respond to the angel based on his relationship with his uncle Abraham. Lot immediately want to meet their needs just as Abraham had done for them prior to his arrival here to Lot. This speaks volume about Lot and what he has learned from his uncle. This should let us know the importance of learning how to engage God based on those we have seen in a position of how to engage God and his Holy vessels in an appropriate manner. Like Abraham he begs them to stay with him for the night. Once they agree, Lot just like Abraham prepares them food and lodging. The interesting thing about this point is I have often heard that we entertain angels unaware. In addition, it amazes me that based on Lot recognizing the angels, he attempts to protect them by bringing them into his home before they are exposed or contaminated by the people in the community. Could it be that we are just not knowledgeable enough to readily recognize God or his angels as did Abraham and Lot? Perhaps it is our responsibility to learn how to engage everyone the same, in the Love of Christ Jesus. The reason I express this point is because if we knew then we would automatically treat them differently from the neighbor across the street.

⁴ But before they lay down, the men of the city, the men of Sodom, both young and old, all the people to the last man, surrounded the house. ⁵ ᵘAnd they called to Lot, "Where are the men who came to you tonight? ᵛBring them out to us, that we ᵂmay know them." ⁶ Lot went out to the men at the entrance, shut the door after him, ⁷ and said, "I beg you, my brothers, do not act so wickedly. ⁸ ˣBehold, I have two daughters who have not known any man. Let me bring them out to you and do to them as you please. Only do nothing to these men, for they have come under the shelter of my roof." ⁹ But they said, "Stand back!" And they said, "This fellow ʸcame to sojourn, and ᶻhe has become the judge! Now we will deal worse with you than with them." Then they pressed hard against the man Lot and drew near to break the door down. ¹⁰ But the men reached out their hands and brought Lot into the house with them and shut the door. ¹¹ And they struck with ᵃblindness the men who were at the entrance of the house, both small and great, so that they wore themselves out groping for the door.

Points to Consider: The interesting thing is God has a conversation with Abraham about the people of Sodom and if he could find 50 good people would he spare the city. We do know that Abraham was thinking of his nephew and his family when he is talking to God about his decision to destroy the city. This means that Abraham had some idea of what life was like in Sodom or at least he had heard about this place. I would imagine his main focused was to save his family from the destruction, while lobbing for others in the city of Sodom to be saved as well.

The bible does not share much with us about the city or people of Sodom other than that God has heard the cries of the people and he was sending his angles to destroy the city of Sodom. This makes you wonder just what in the world is going on in Sodom that God has heard the voices of his people and is about to destroy the city. Baring this information in mind we know that if God has sent word to destroy the city it must be extremely corrupt. For example, the text shows that Lot has met the physical needs of the angels and that they have eaten well. The angels are now preparing to lay down for the night and suddenly there is a call out to Lot for the men. In addition, we see here that all the people were drawn to Lot's house even unto the very last man. Now we can begin to start developing a sense of where the minds of the men of Sodom were along with their intentions. The question then becomes why is that all the men of Sodom have waited until now to seek out the men and what is it that they really want, and why? Based on the cries of the people and God giving the angels orders to destroy the city one must conclude that all the men have gathered outside of Lot's house with bad intentions.

The scriptures states that all the men surround Lots house where the angels were. I often wonder why they could not recognize that these were not ordinary men but instead angels. Perhaps their minds were fixated and so morally corrupt that they could only see what they wanted and clearly it was these two men who just happens to be angels. The bible makes it known that the people did not recognize them to be angels or so it is not stated that they did; however, we see they are drawn to the men like vultures drawn to prey.

The people only recognize them to be men who were new to the city. Reminds me of when a new girl comes to town all the boys are drawn to her and want to get a good look at her to see who will be the one that wins her over. In this case the men of Sodom make it noticeably clear what their intentions for the new men in the city were. I would imagine that this was a rather common set of circumstances. I am confident that this is what the cries from the people to God were all about.

Lot tries to convince the men to leave the men alone and to not act so wickedly. The statement by Lot lets us further know that Lot knew exactly what was about to go down. I often ask myself if Lot knew how the men acted in this city why not leave this city. Why would Lot want to live in such an environment and to allow his family to live in such a city? My question is had Lot become a product of this environment. The text does not articulate that, but one would have to assume that though he may not have participated in such wicked action is very aware of what goes down in the city and how the men get down. Lot immediately want to shield them from the community by getting the men in and out as quickly as possible because he knew all too well what goes on after dark in Sodom. Did Lot have to succomb to these same advances upon his arrival? If so, how did he handle this situation? Was Lot given a pass not to be subjected to these homosexual advances to sleep with all the men in the city? How horrible and wicked is this set of circumstances for anyone to have to try and go through. Where were the women of the city? Perhaps they were the ones praying and it was their cries that God. There is no record of them. The men of this city actions appear normal and quite possibly customary in the city of Sodom. Was this an eye opener for Lot and his family to finally see the truth? Lots of questions no real answers to this mystery.

The text clearly state the men of Sodom intentions are to know the men. So, what does it mean to know them? We collect information about what it means to know them based on what Lot articulates to the men gathered outside of his house. The bible does not clearly say that the men want to have sex with the angels, but Lot makes it very plain. The interesting thing is we see here that not just one man or two men, but all the men of Sodom has plans on having sex with the men under Lots roof. This information makes it much clearer as to why God wants to destroy this city. There is something very unnatural and very wicked going on in the city of Sodom. The men of this city and their intentions for anyone traveling to or in this city.

The next part becomes very puzzling to me for several reason but especially me as a father. Lot is so desperate to convince the men to leave the two angels alone that he offers his two daughters to them. Then Lot goes further to say you can do as you please with them. Wow that is shocking. This father offer's his two virgin daughters to a mob of men. A mob of men who I believe Lot was well aware of their capabilities based on his firsthand experience living next to these men every day. He does this all in the hopes that the men of the city would agree and leave the two angels alone but to no avail. I believe if the men of Sodom are willing to turn down Lots two virgin daughters to whom he was freely offering to them the problem is much greater than we know. Think about it Lot offers his two daughters to them to do with as they pleased. The men did not want women and it is obvious that these men crave homosexual relationships, and they did not want a woman. Lot steps out the house shouts the door behind him and begs the men not to do this. The men become angry with Lot and say who made you a judge of us. The men then threaten Lot and say bring them out to us and if you do not, we will do worst with you. This story gets progressively worst. Lot is in a really bad situation with his neighbors who he lives next to in the same community. Lot knows that the men of the city wanted to be with other men. This can be conclude based on their response to Lots gracious offer.

Things have gotten so bad that the men of Sodom are about to break the door down so the angels grab Lot shuts the door and causes the men of Sodom to go blind. The men were still trying to get to the angles by groping them. Now that is bad. You have been stricken blind and you still trying to get to the men. Seems like they would just give up, call it a night and go home but they continued after the two angels. I can envision it as I type and read. This is so awful who would be this desperate and wicked to do such things. I am beginning to understand why God is going to destroy the city. The men were clearly wicked and determined to do as they please to whomever they pleased.

[12] Then the men said to Lot, "Have you anyone else here? Sons-in-law, sons, daughters, or anyone you have in the city, [b]bring them out of the place. [13] For we are about to destroy this place, [c]because the outcry against its people has become great before the LORD, and the LORD has sent us to destroy it." [14] So Lot went out and said to his sons-in-law, who were to marry his daughters, [d]"Up! Get out of this place, for the LORD is about to destroy the city." But he seemed to his sons-in-law to be jesting.

Points to Consider: Look at God's grace and mercy for the prayers of Abraham and the Love he has for Lot does not go unnoticed by God. God reveals to Lot what is about to happen and offers him a warning. God is given Lot the opportunity to get his family and leave rather than be destroyed along with the city. We discover there is something wrong here with Lots relationships. What type of relationship did Lot have with his two future son-in- laws? What we do know is, that they would not take heed to his warnings and leave the city? They figure Lot is just joking. What does this say about Lot?

[15] As morning dawned, the angels urged Lot, saying, "Up! Take your wife and your two daughters who are here, lest you be swept away in the punishment of the city." [16] But he lingered. So the men seized him and his wife and his two daughters by the hand, [e]the LORD being merciful to him, and they brought him out and set him outside the city. [17] And as they brought them out, one said, "Escape for your life. [f]Do not look back or stop anywhere in the [g]valley. Escape to the hills, lest you be swept away." [18] And Lot said to them, "Oh, no, my lords. [19] Behold, your servant has found favor in your sight, and you have shown me great kindness in saving my life. But I cannot escape to the hills, lest the disaster overtake me and I die. [20] Behold, this city is near enough to flee to, and it is a little one. Let me escape there—is it not a little one?—and my life will be saved!" [21] He said to him, "Behold, I grant you this favor also, that I will not overthrow the city of which you have

spoken. [22] Escape there quickly, for I can do nothing till you arrive there." Therefore the name of the city was called ᵸZoar.ᴸ

Points to Consider: We see that morning was drawing near and the angels must encourage Lot to get moving, take your wife and two daughters who are here with him right now. They tell Lot you better go now before you and your family are punished right along with the rest of the people in the city. The alarming thing about this whole event is why in the world does the angels have to urge motivate or encourage you to leave after you already know the reason why the angels are in your home.

The text does not go into great detail about what was the hold up on Lot, but it does say that the angels had to seized Lot and the whole family by the hand and practically drag them out of the house and the city. This makes no sense to me at all. What was the hold up? Did they want to die along with the rest of the people? Were they all so tied to the city that they were not able to get together to leave. I mean the angles had to grab them by the hand and jerk them out of the city because they were not in a rush or hurry even though they knew that God was going to destroy the city. This is utterly ridiculous to me. God's grace and mercy being extended to the point where he wanted to ensure that Abraham's family was in complete safety before he destroyed Sodom.

I am so amazed at Gods mercy towards Lot based on Gods relationship with his uncle Abraham. This lets me further understand the impact of having a relationship with God and the importance of your family relationship with God. I mean when examining this story we see Lot appears to be just messing around during a state of emergency. Lots actions are completely puzzling. I mean why doesn't he have a sense of urgency to get him and his family out of this wicked city. Then we see the angels providing direction to Lot, but his response is not good. The angles say run for your life, head for the hills, and do not look back. Simple instructions or at least it seems as if it should be simple.

What I have discovered in reading and gaining understanding about Lot's personality and behavior is that Lot's thinking was way off. Here is why I say that, first he lives in a very wicked city and he is completely okay living in such a wicked city. Lot knows how new people are treated by the men in the city when they come into the city. At least the men are treated this way based on what we have learned via the text. We know that Lot is not a poor man, because the scriptures tells us that he cut ties with Abraham his uncle who we know was a very wealthy man because together they had so much wealth including servants that the need to separate was inevitable. The servants began to argue. To have servants meant you had wealth. This is how Lot separates from his uncle and lands in Sodom. Did Lot lose his wealth and all his servants and had no other option but to stay in Sodom. Was he now in poverty and could not move? The reason I pose this question is because based on my personal experience most people would leave a bad environment or in this case a very wicked community if they have the money or resources to do so. So why does Lot subject his family to living under such conditions. Lot by his own admission recognizes that the men of the city are wicked.

Moving forward why Lot listens to the three simple instructions run for your life, do not look back and run to the hills. In examining the text, we recognize that he had no sense of urgency to leave the city. We recognize this based on the angles having to pull him and his entire family by the hands because they were not moving with urgency. The angles offer him extremely specific directions such as run for your life and run to the hills. So, move quickly because life depends on it and go to the hills. The angels give him a safe place to go; however, he negotiates with them to go somewhere else. Not good at all. Why doesn't he just listen rather than trying to go somewhere else? I am thinking if this was me, I would not be going anywhere but to my uncle Abraham's house if I do not go to the hills as directed to do so. This decision comes back to haunt Lot and his two daughters in the end. You will have to read on and finish this story to find out. I told you the bible is better than any reality TV or soap opera any day.

The instruction not to look back causes Lot's wife to tragically loose her life even after God saved her from the city. The funny thing is we do not even know her name; she is only known as Lot's wife. I would think that since the angels said run for your life and do not look back that they would be moving with great hast and too busy getting out of there to take time and turn back, but Lots wife does turn and look back. This action cause two daughters to lose their mother and Lot to lose his wife. Why does she look back? This question has always been puzzling to me. We know from our study that the city was wicked, we know that the men of the city would force themselves on other men without permission. The men obviously did not bother women because Lot has two daughters who are still virgins. Why is this? Why haven't the men forced themselves on to their daughters? Puzzling to say the least! So, what was life like in the city of Sodom for Lot's wife? The scripture does not tell us, but what it does tell us, is that she is the only one who turns and looks back and immediately turns into a pillar of salt and dies. This lets us know further that she had some sort of soul ties to the city as well. One the houses was only so big so she is aware of what is about to go down in the city. She is forced along with the rest of the family to get out now, but the angel pulled by the hand, gives her instructions, but still she stops, turns back and looks on Sodom. The answer to this question we may never know; however, it is my experience that when someone looks back on something, they are forced to be left back. She had some sort of regret or longing to go back based on something that she longed for or missed. Continue reading the story below for the details of what happens to Lot's wife, the city and the enormous Love God has for Abraham and his family.

God Destroys Sodom

²³ The sun had risen on the earth when Lot came to Zoar. ²⁴ Then ⁱthe LORD rained on Sodom and Gomorrah sulfur and fire from the LORD out of heaven. ²⁵ And he overthrew those cities, and all the valley, and all the inhabitants of the cities, and what grew on the ground. ²⁶ But Lot's wife, behind him, looked back, and she became ^ja pillar of salt.

²⁷ And Abraham went early in the morning to the place where he had ^kstood before the LORD. ²⁸ And he looked down toward Sodom and Gomorrah and toward all the land of the valley, and he looked and, behold, the smoke of the land went up like the smoke of a furnace.

²⁹ So it was that, when God destroyed the cities of the valley, God ^lremembered Abraham and sent Lot out of the midst of the overthrow when he overthrew the cities in which Lot had lived.

Points to Consider: Being a product of your environment has generational impacts

Research is constantly being done and has been done to determine the future or the life of others. Various research studies that do support gaining understanding of your family dynamics is important to your future. In order to understand who we are we often must look at the character traits of our parents and grandparents. In addition to understand who we are we must consider our surroundings and the effects of the people we are in direct contact with on a regular basis. Our community at large and the people in our communities play an incredibly significant role in our life. This happens no matter how we try to avoid the impact. In this next set of scriptures, we will see just how much of our thinking is altered by our parents and community at large.

Our surroundings and the people we encounter do play a huge role in our lives. The byproduct of your environment has long been used when determining outcomes for the life of people. We often look at where a person is from to determine where or how he or she may end up. A perfect example would be the way of thinking of children to their parents. You will notice that children often take on the mindset of their parents. Normally this happens through social modeling, in depth conversations that revolve around their families' morals and values. What they feel is important. This is normally based on familiarity to our parents and how they speak, think or respond. No matter how we try to avoid thinking like or being like our parents often times we become or think just like them or similar to the thinking of them. This why it is important that we take on the mind of Christ Jesus rather than that of our parents or community. We see this all playing out in this next set of scriptures. Let us look at how the impact of Lot's thinking and growing up in Sodom has impacted the thinking of Lot's two daughters.

Lot and His Daughters

30 Now Lot went up out of Zoar and m lived in the hills with his two daughters, for he was afraid to live in Zoar. So he lived in a cave with his two daughters. 31 And the firstborn said to the younger, "Our father is old, and there is not a man on earth to come in to us after the manner of all the earth. 32 Come, let us make our father drink wine, and we will lie with him, that we may preserve offspring from our father." 33 So they made their father drink wine that night. And the firstborn went in and lay with her father. He did not know when she lay down or when she arose.

34 The next day, the firstborn said to the younger, "Behold, I lay last night with my father. Let us make him drink wine tonight also. Then you go in and lie with him, that we may preserve offspring from our father." 35 So they made their father drink wine that night also. And the younger arose

and lay with him, and he did not know when she lay down or when she arose. [36] Thus both the daughters of Lot became pregnant by their father. [37] The firstborn bore a son and called his name Moab.[2] [n]He is the father of the Moabites to this day. [38] The younger also bore a son and called his name Ben-ammi.[3] [o]He is the father of the Ammonites to this day.

Points to Consider: In our last interactions with Lot, he does not want to go to the hills as directed by the two angels. Lot insist on going to Zoar. Why we do not know, but he attempts to persuade the angles to let him go there rather than to the Hills. We can assume something has happened because now we find him in the hills rather than in the city of choice. Lot initially says he does not want to go there for fear of being over taken and the angels agreed to allow him to go. Once he arrives it is noted that God then destroys Sodom. This clearly indicate Gods love for him.

Lot is currently living in the hills with his two daughters. Remember his wife is dead because she looked back and was turned into a pillar of salt. So, it is just Lot and his two daughters living in the hills. The text states he now afraid to live in Zoar. This statement shows that Lot has quite a few issues going on with him. Could Lot have an intellectual disability or just be so impacted from living in Sodom and being forced to live because God destroyed and know he is a mental wreck. We do know he was apparently pretty comfortable or at least stable while in Sodom, which is very bazar.

Up until this part we do not hear from the daughters they are just mentioned as Lots daughters. The daughter's names are not mentioned and is never mentioned like that of their mother. One would think that they are good kids based on the fact they do not offer any push back. We do know that they were not moving with any since of urgency to leave Sodom. We also learn that the two daughters are engaged to be married. Unfortunately, we learn that the two fiancées are destroyed along with the city because they did not take heed to Lot's warning. The two men figured Lot was joking which is weird. Weird because they did not have enough respect for Lot to take heed to his warning. Their lack of response to Lot cost them their lives to include Lots inability to have influence on his future son in Laws.

We see here that Lot's daughters thinking is a bit off. They have great intentions, but a very warp way of carrying their intentions out. Initially studying this text, it used to puzzle me because I often wondered what would make his two daughters come to this conclusion. Now on the other hand I realize that there is more going on than I initially understood. Praise the Lord. I see it differently now after much prayer and studying. Looking at their parents' thinking and the thinking of the city that they have grown up in it makes total sense as why they thought that what they were doing was good when really, they were doing evil based on my learning and experiences. In fact, I think it is imperative that we take in consideration on what we discover initially about Lots' first statement involving his two daughters. I believe this is too important not to high light at this point in the story. Lot is willing to give them to the wicked men. I am sure the daughters had to hear their father offering them up as a sacrifice to the men of the city of Sodom to do with them as they please. I am not sure if this statement had some real damaging impact on the two daughters. I happen to believe they had to feel like wow my dad who is my protector and provider has just decided to toss us off to the men of Sodom even though we are already spoken for how our father could love strangers more than he loves his own daughters. This is just my thinking. Did they have the capacity to even understand why their father was making this decision?

The interesting point here is we see they think that now we have no options to reproduce other than to sleep with their father to preserve their offspring. Let us review just what the daughters are saying again, "And the firstborn said to the younger, "Our father is old, and there is not a man on earth to come in to us after the manner of all the earth. [32]

Come, let us make our father drink wine, and we will lie with him, that we may preserve offspring from our father." The next day, the firstborn said to the younger, "Behold, I lay last night with my father. Let us make him drink wine tonight, also. Then you go in and lie with him, that we may preserve offspring from our father." ³⁵So they made their father drink wine that night also. And the younger arose and lay with him, and he did not know when she lay down or when she arose. ³⁶ Thus both the daughters of Lot became pregnant by their father. ³³ So they made their father drink wine that night. And the firstborn went in and lay with her father. He did not know when she lay down or when she arose."

Although Abraham lobbies to God to spare his family's life we must recognize that there had to be something seriously wrong with Lot and his wife to remain in such a city when he could have easily gone back to stay with his uncle Abraham. We discover Lot never tries to reconnect with his uncle Abraham. I often wondered why? Why go live in a cave only with your two daughters? These actions we should not be surprised at, but we are. So now we are briefly introducing how they think. The question is why they would they think that there are no other men on the whole earth to marry and reproduce with. One would think that they had to be pretty sheltered or there was something missing or maybe they thought that God had destroyed the whole world, one could only imagine what their thoughts were.

Wow, what a wicked plan to come up with but we must remember they grew up in a wicked city. They may have been destroyed but the influences and impact the city had on Lot's daughters would last long after the city was destroyed. Looking back on Lot's decision not to return to Abraham was the best decision he could have made. One can only imagine the impact his presence and influence would have made on Abraham's household.

The interesting point here is they at least I know that Lot would not agree with their actions in good conscience or when he was of sober mind. I imagine that is why they made the decision to get their father drunk. I do want to point out that it was the oldest daughter's idea originally and she had already committed the act and then enticed her sister to do the same thing. I often wondered just how much they gave him to drink considering he was so drunk he does not remember anything that happened. I am not a drinker so I cannot empathize here, however this is such a puzzling set of circumstances for me. I also wonder how Lot's daughters knew that this idea would even work. This clearly shows that their thinking was completely off, based on them believing this was their only option was to have offspring.

When running from God goes wrong- Points to Consider

This is an incredibly interesting story, and most people are remarkably familiar with this story. The story has been told repeatedly for centuries. The funny thing is, the story has been mostly shared in a fairy tale type format. The story is enlightening and intriguing. The problem with this story is, that it just does not seem real even though its told in churches all over the world. From the beginning to the end of the story it is so amazing that hardly anyone who hears it finds it to be true or even believable. This is one of the reasons I chose this story to talk about, study and explore in hopes that God will reveal something special for each reader to see and understand better than before.

The story begins with Now the word of the Lord came to Jonah the son of Amittai saying, get up now and go to Nineveh that great city and call out against it for the evil in the city has come up before me. We see a classic case of someone who out right refuses to carry out God's instructions. My question has always been why God chose him and why he would even attempt to try and run from God. The very notions just seem totally absurd, even though we have all done it in some form or fashion.

In this story, there are just so many unanswered questions. What we do know is God listens to the prayers of his people and knows everything going on with him. This is yet another perfect example of how much God really loves us, cares about us, and actually listens and responds to our prayers. He also knows who can and cannot carry out what he has directed them to do. The crazy part is, if he says we should just follow it with blind faith, even if we do not believe we can. In this case, we see God references his father. I would venture to say that perhaps God was trying to get him to step and be like his father. I am not sure why his father's name is referenced here but let us read below what is happening in his life.

Jonah Flees the Presence of the Lord

1 Now the word of the LORD came to Jonah the son of Amittai, saying, [2] "Arise, go to Nineveh, that great city, and call out against it, for their evil[a] has come up before me." [3] But Jonah rose to flee to Tarshish from the presence of the LORD. He went down to Joppa and found a ship going to Tarshish. So, he paid the fare and went down into it, to go with them to Tarshish, away from the presence of the LORD.

[4] But the LORD hurled a great wind upon the sea, and there was a mighty tempest on the sea, so that the ship threatened to break up. [5] Then the mariners were afraid, and each cried out to his god. And they hurled the cargo that was in the ship into the sea to lighten it for them. But Jonah had gone down into the inner part of the ship and had lain down and was fast asleep. [6] So the captain came and said to him, "What do you mean, you sleeper? Arise, call out to your god! Perhaps the god will give a thought to us, that we may not perish."

Points to Consider: The call from God comes directly to Jonah to immediately go to Nineveh and speak against its sin. Seems like a clear and precise directive straight from God. However, my question is just how much he knows about God at this point in his life. The reason I ask this question is because of his response to what God has directed him to do. Seems very odd to me that he would respond this way to an almighty God in this manner. Was this his first personal experience hearing from God? What had his relationship been like with God at this point, and what makes him believe he can run away from God? I would imagine he had heard enough about God to know that there is nowhere you can run that you would be away from the presences of God or at least he finds out the hard way.

The interesting thing about this situation is we look and judge Jonah at this point harshly, but I wonder how many times God has directed us to go and speak to someone and we refused. God is always giving us urges to go and do and we run completely away from his directive similar to that of Jonah. God may not have asked you or I to go speak to a capital city like Nineveh, but he does ask us to go and speak to our neighbors and coworkers. So I ask, before we attack him lets empathize with him just for a moment. Now, think on this for a moment often have we and do we flee from these simple instructions from God. Looking at the test at hand for Jonah it really is a big test. The city of Nineveh was the capital city, and it was a vast and thriving city on the move. To make it more visible to each reader. Think about New York or Atlanta as an example of a modern Nineveh. However, no matter how big or powerful the city may be we see that the city's sins have come up before God and God has selected Jonah to go and speak against the city. The scripture does not necessarily say that Jonah is afraid, but we can just assume based on his response to God that he was so afraid of the city that he disobeyed God. What makes him more afraid of the city than disobeying God? Whatever that rationale was we see the power of fear is at work here?

So, Jonah goes and quickly purchase him a ticket and jumps on the boat. The boat is going in the opposite direction from where God has asked him to go. Jonah is thinking he can jump on a boat and totally get away from God. Wow, we see here that leaving the presence of God is not possible and it could lead to deadly consequences. So, he goes down to the inner part of the boat and goes to sleep. He wakes up to utter devastation because God has hurled a great wind upon the sea. The sea becomes overwhelmingly rough and now threatens to break the ship into. The wind, the sea, and the people have all been affected based on one man's decision to try and flee from God with no success. The people are throwing things over board to lighten the load of the ship. I am sure these things are unbelievably valuable and filled with purpose and that is why they are even on the ship. We see that everyone has been demanded to call on their god to see if their god would rescue them. So, we see Jonah at ease chilling at the bottom of the boat sleeping peacefully while holy chaos is going on up above.

The people working the boat were very experienced sea men. In fact they were mariners so we know that they were experienced and had various experience with heavy wind storm before. What they discovered, was no ordinary sea storm. The winds God sent were so mighty and devastating that it was completely overwhelming to most experienced seaman. They were overwhelmed to the point that, they decided to throw all the expensive cargo over Board. These men were desperate because their lives depended on it. Then when that does not appear to be working, we see that they realized that something much more powerful is a work here. The captain recognized that the only way we are going to survive this wind is if we pray and pray right now. This is the appropriate response however they served many gods and had no clue which god was at work here.

I can envision the captain as he comes upon Jonah who he does not even know by name, but he sees him below the deck sleeping and chilling while everyone else is running around scrambling based on the weather conditions. I can imagine how he must feel here we are doing everything we can to survive and this guy is below deck sound asleep. The captain in his panic calls him a sleeper. The captain is furious and afraid all at the same time, so he says to Jonah, "What do you mean, you sleeper? Arise, call out to your god! Perhaps the god will give a thought to us that we may not perish." We do know that although the captain is not a believer because he basically says we do not know what god this is that is causing this storm, but we know it is not a natural storm. The captain out of desperation identifies that he as a seaman had never experienced this type of storm before. The captain wants it to stop. I am sure he is running around like a chicken with his head chopped off asking everyone he sees to pray to their god in hopes that they all maybe saved. When the captain of the boat is afraid there is a real problem going on. I can only imagine the chaos taking place with the boat, the crew and the people on board the boat and Jonah is below chilling fast asleep. Wow, interesting let us keep reading there is still yet so much more to learn from this story.

I begin the book talking about people being in their feelings. We see here that the captain was really in his feelings. The captain does not really care what God saves them, he just knows this situation is unreal, and it is not going to end well without divine intervention. I can only imagine what the crew is thinking. Remember we have experienced seamen here working hard to survive. The captain along with his men have been through many of severe storms while at sea before I'm sure. What we do know is those past storms don't compare with this one from God. The captain and all the crew are extremely terrified and really do not know what to do in this situation, we see them acting out of utter desperation. They are so afraid that they are willing to do anything to save their lives. Fear will cause you to be confused and all up in your feelings. Fear definitely heightens your emotional level and before you know it you're an emotional wreck.

Jonah Is Thrown into the Sea

⁷ And they said to one another, "Come, let us cast lots, that we may know on whose account this evil has come upon us." So, they cast lots, and the lot fell on Jonah. ⁸ Then they said to him, "Tell us on whose account this evil has come upon us. What is your occupation? And where do you come from? What is your country? And of what people are you?" ⁹ And he said to them, "I am a Hebrew, and I fear the Lord, the God of heaven, who made the sea and the dry land." ¹⁰ Then the men were exceedingly afraid and said to him, "What is this that you have done!" For the men knew that he was fleeing from the presence of the Lord, because he had told them.

Points to Consider: The men are so desperate that they begin to cast lots to try and figure out who is responsible for this evil that has come upon them. How do these men even come to this conclusion to even think to cast lots? I am thinking to myself how is casting lots going to give them the answer that they are seeking? How logical or practical is this? We see here again that everyone can plainly identify that this is no ordinary storm, and they plan to get to the bottom of this situation immediately. Interestingly enough the casting of lots actually works and it lands on the right person Jonah. I am thinking to myself how valid or reliable is the lots test that they will allow this to determine their decisions or fate.

The men instantly begin to quiz Jonah in an attempt to get to the bottom of this life-or-death situation that they are currently facing. The men pose some noticeably clear and precise questions to solve this mystery. Then they said to him, "Tell us on whose account this evil has come upon us. What is your occupation? And where do you come from? What is your country? And of what people are you? As shocking are the men's questions his response is equally as alarming, he has a choice to make whether or not to tell the truth. Remember he is already afraid, and he is running away from the presence of God out of fear of doing what God has called him to do. We see him being trapped now between God and Man. To make matters worse he is at sea this time and there is nowhere to run and nowhere to hide. He is now forced to face his fears.

Truth has revealed, and confirmed this is not an ordinary storm it is a supernatural storm from the Hebrew God. What is extremely interesting is what he reveals next in his description of his God. Jonah states, "I am a Hebrew, and I fear the Lord, the God of heaven, who made the sea and the dry land."[10] Then the men were exceedingly afraid and said to him, "What is this that you have done!" For the men knew that he was fleeing from the presence of the Lord, because he had told them. The only thing I can say at this point of the story is wow what an entanglement he finds himself in.

[11] Then they said to him, "What shall we do to you, that the sea may quiet down for us?" For the sea grew more and more tempestuous. [12] He said to them, "Pick me up and hurl me into the sea; then the sea will quiet down for you, for I know it is because of me that this great tempest has come upon you." [13] Nevertheless, the men rowed hard[b] to get back to dry land, but they could not, for the sea grew more and more tempestuous against them. [14] Therefore they called out to the LORD, "O LORD, let us not perish for this man's life, and lay not on us innocent blood, for you, O LORD, have done as it pleased you." [15] So they picked up Jonah and hurled him into the sea, and the sea ceased from its raging. [16] Then the men feared the LORD exceedingly, and they offered a sacrifice to the LORD and made vows.

Points to Consider: Desperate times calls for desperate measures. I find it very odd that they would ask him what we shall do to you that the sea may quiet down for us. For the sea grew more and more tempestuous. Meaning the heat is turning up even more now. What to do in this dilemma? I do not know what I would have done. Do you know what you would do in this situation? I guess it is easy for any of us to say what we would or could do after reading this powerful story. I do not believe I would have allowed what Jonah said to come out of my mouth. In fact, we see here Jonah becomes bold or at least in this current dynamic he does by telling the men to throw me over board. I can think of a lot of other things to say other than throw me over board. I mean like I would have said let us all get down on our knees and pray and repent but throwing me overboard just is not on the tip of my tongue. What is he thinking? Is he now ready to commit suicide because he is so afraid? How does he even come to this conclusion? Does he somehow increase his faith and believe that God will rescue him if the men toss him in the sea as he suggests?

This idea of throwing him overboard did not initially sit too well with the men or the captain because rather than throw him overboard as he suggest, the men try to continue to row the boat to shore for safety. Could it be that the men were too afraid to risk further risk of death? Did the men have a greater moral compass or what, or was this response out of fear of making the wrong decision? I would like to think it was because they did not want to make the wrong decision and have the Hebrew God destroy them.

Look at this, we see a drastic change happening here. What we do know is that the men were convinced that this was not a natural disaster and definitely a divine order from God. The men knew that they had to be wise in their responses to this life-or-death matter. The men also knew that this was the most powerful display of supernatural occurrences that had happened in their lives. This experience brought about a change in the lives of these men forever. I also believe the men are now convinced of who the one true living God is based on their next action. Look at the reaction of the men at this point and what happens, therefore they called out to the Lord, "O Lord, let us not perish for this man's life, and lay not on us innocent blood, for you, O Lord, have done as it pleased you." [15] So they picked up Jonah and hurled him into the sea, and the sea ceased from its raging. [16] Then the men feared the Lord exceedingly, and they offered a sacrifice to the Lord and made vows.

I could imagine the sigh of relief the men had to have experience to see the raging sea instantly calm down after tossing Jonah into the sea. The men took a chance but prayed and asked God first for favor not to destroy them. The men then made a sacrifice to God and made a vow to the Lord. This traumatic incident has cause men's lives to change forever. Once upon a time, these seaman believed in many gods now we see them make vows to the true and living God. This experience has already been amazing and for the greater good of changing men's lives for the better. We see that not only has this running from God trip affect Jonah's life for the better we see the unlimited opportunities for the lives of these men and their families be changed. Remember these are men who travel the sea and wherever they go they will forever tell this story of how the raging sea was calmed by the Hebrew God. I believe the lives of everyone they came in contact with believe in God after they shared their experience with them. Until this study, I never saw how impactful this one experience could have changed the lives of so many others.

In Gods great plan for our lives, we rarely see the huge impact that one decision could potentially have on so many other people. We see in this part of the story that Jonah recognizes that not only is his life being altered based on his decision not to obey God but the life of so many others. I believe if and when we have the capacity to comprehend and retain this for ourselves, we would see the big picture. The big picture is that God wants all men saved and protected and everything is not always just about us and how we feel about something. We have so many people tied to us. We can see here that these men do not want innocent blood on their hands, so they ask for forgiveness if this decision that they are making is wrong. There is a large sum of innocence to their request and I believe God honored their actions because we see that the raging sea instantly calmed down. This life-or-death situation has now been brought under control.

A Great Fish Swallows Jonah

17 [c] And the LORD appointed[d] a great fish to swallow up Jonah. And Jonah was in the belly of the fish three days and three nights.

Points to Consider: So, we have not seen the last of Jonah. We see God doing what he does showing his people kindness and mercy even when perhaps we do not deserve it. I mean Jonah asked to be tossed overboard into a raging sea without a prayer or a plan. Wow, talking about being in your feelings. Should he have not said let me pray first? Think about it if you know you are already in a deadly storm and you just asked to be thrown overboard in the storm, would you want to at least pray first. I know I would or even if he forgot the men who were not believers even, they prayed before tossing him overboard. He could have simply followed their example.

God appoints a fish to swallow up Jonah. This is quite remarkable and the part that is often the piece of the story that defies logic for me. Even this day unless you have experience or understand the power that God has this is so unreal. The interesting thing is we were all probably introduce to this story as a kid in Sunday school or some Christian school and we have heard the story repeatedly but have we ever just studied the story. Like I am wondering now, God assigned a great fish to swallow up Jonah and then why was he in there for three days? Three days seems to me to be an exceptionally long time. Then I realized that Jonah ran from the presence of the Lord on Land, Sea and now he must sit in the belly of a whale for three long days. Was he there that long to realize that no matter where he ran God would be there? This is a tough lesson to learn but we know from this study that Jonah was pretty hard headed and he was a runner. Now he is stuck in the whale's belly with no place to run or hide.

Jonah 2 English Standard Version (ESV)

Jonah's Prayer

2 Then Jonah prayed to the LORD his God from the belly of the fish, [2] saying,"I called out to the LORD, out of my distress, and he answered me; out of the belly of Sheol I cried,

and you heard my voice.[3] For you cast me into the deep,

into the heart of the seas, and the flood surrounded me;

all your waves and your billows passed over me.[4] Then I said, 'I am driven away

from your sight; yet I shall again look upon your holy temple.'

[5] The waters closed in over me to take my life; the deep surrounded me;

weeds were wrapped about my head [6] at the roots of the mountains. I went down to the land

whose bars closed upon me forever; yet you brought up my life from the pit,

O LORD my God.[7] When my life was fainting away,

I remembered the LORD, and my prayer came to you,

into your holy temple.[8] Those who pay regard to vain idols

forsake their hope of steadfast love.[9] But I with the voice of thanksgiving

will sacrifice to you; what I have vowed I will pay.

Salvation belongs to the LORD!"[10] And the LORD spoke to the fish, and it vomited Jonah out upon the dry land.

Points to Consider: Now after reading what Jonah experienced, I see why God allowed him to go through this way. God knew from the very beginning how Jonah would respond, but he chose to use him anyway. We see Jonah almost allowed his fears to rob him of his destiny. I also realize that there were others lives affected by Jonah, so he had to go this way. This way seems hard but the more and more I understand I realize that there are those of us who will not readily accept our call or direction based on the size of the call, and this was a big call God placed on his life.

The call was so heavy on Jonah that he does not consider his actions to be optional. He feels he must run for his life to flee the presence of God. He finds himself on a boat in a deadly storm. He now goes from a deadly storm to being tossed in a violent sea. This appears to be the end for him, and he seems to have embraced his result. The good thing or the great thing is he is being cared for by the almighty God. God sends him a personal savior in the form of a large fish, where he remains for three days alone. This is the first time we see him totally alone with his thoughts and of course guess who? God of course. There is a shift in thoughts as we see or hear his description of his journey while in the sea. Jonah has a complete change in his thoughts. I believe he now finally recognizes that there is no running from God. Based on his actions he is given an opportunity to experience God on a whole different level. He sees God's power quite different now. He sees the vastness of God's power directly in the wind, the sea and now the animals. What kind of God is this? Jonah went from running from land to sea only to discover there is nowhere to run and nowhere to hide from God. God's power is ultimate, and it rains supreme.

Jonah for the first time in this experience is stuck in one place with his thoughts and look at what he now realizes. After his many attempts to run away from God. Look at his prayer to God. There is a total shift in mind here. The near-death experience has totally changed his prospective for the better. I guess there is nothing like a life-threatening experience to realize just how real God is and how powerful he is as well. The three days allowed him time to reflect on all the recent events that have happened in his most recent experiences with God. The experiences leave him with life changing thoughts while siting in the belly of the fish. I can imagine him thinking his life has come to an end and he probably has no clue where he really is, but he recognizes the need to pray. The thought of prayer never seemed to cross his mind or at least it is not documented anywhere even when he heard non believers praying, he still never utters a word of prayer.

I imagine him sitting on the tongue of the whale hungry, depressed, and angry. Every emotion known to man is now going through his mind. I am certain there are tons of what ifs that have crossed his mind. How did I get here? Will I ever make it out? Whatever his thoughts or questions we see he finally turns to God and pray. Man, this is one stubborn person. I have never heard of anyone being this stubborn before in the scriptures to the point you end up siting in the belly of a fish. I would imagine him being very afraid and lonely and he now longs for the presence of God. What a great mind set to finally arrive at where he desires to be in God's presence now? We recognize that based on his prayer to God; the text teaches us that after he prays God speaks to the fish and directs him to vomit him out on dry land. This is remarkable. I often think, man, could he have just followed God's instruction from the beginning? Perhaps he could have, but I would imagine now he is determined to follow Gods direction despite his feelings.

Jonah 3 English Standard Version (ESV)

Jonah Goes to Nineveh

3 Then the word of the LORD came to Jonah the second time, saying, [2] "Arise, go to Nineveh, that great city, and call out against it the message that I tell you." [3] So Jonah arose and went to Nineveh, according to the

word of the LORD. Now Nineveh was an exceedingly great city,[a] three days' journey in breadth.[b] ⁴ Jonah began to go into the city, going a day's journey. And he called out, "Yet forty days, and Nineveh shall be overthrown!" ⁵ And the people of Nineveh believed God. They called for a fast and put on sackcloth, from the greatest of them to the least of them.

The People of Nineveh Repent

⁶ The word reached[c] the king of Nineveh, and he arose from his throne, removed his robe, covered himself with sackcloth, and sat in ashes. ⁷ And he issued a proclamation and published through Nineveh, "By the decree of the king and his nobles: Let neither man nor beast, herd nor flock, taste anything. Let them not feed or drink water, ⁸ but let man and beast be covered with sackcloth, and let them call out mightily to God. Let everyone turn from his evil way and from the violence that is in his hands. ⁹ Who knows? God may turn and relent and turn from his fierce anger, so that we may not perish."

¹⁰ When God saw what they did, how they turned from their evil way, God relented of the disaster that he had said he would do to them, and he did not do it.

Points to Consider: Finally, we see Jonah doing the work God wanted him to do that he so desperately ran from. The response is overwhelmingly shocking. Jonah was on his journey to do the work of the Lord and the people from the richest to the poorest to include the king all responded to the warning from God. The king even went so far as to issue a proclamation to the entire city. The statement stated, a proclamation and published through Nineveh, "By the decree of the king and his nobles: Let neither man nor beast, herd nor flock, taste anything. Let them not feed or drink water, ⁸ but let man and beast be covered with sackcloth and let them call out mightily to God. Let everyone turn from his evil ways and from the violence that is in his hands. [9] Who knows? God may turn and relent and turn from his fierce anger, so that we may not perish."

This response is perfect. This is just what you want the people and especially the king to do. The king makes everyone stop in their tracks repent and stop doing evil, even down to the animals. I do not think I have ever heard this before. The animals had to wear sack cloths. The king means business, everyone is going to repent even the animals. Wow, I am speechless. I cannot remember anyone ever highlight this response. My last book is called responding to the call and I must say this is truly responding to the call of God.

The people all responded to the words of Jonah because they believed God. I never remember reading how quickly the people repented. I mean Jonah went through so much to run away from this assignment only to have the assignment to be so much easier than anyone could imagine. I mean he had to be tossed overboard into a raging sea and on top of that he had to spend three days and nights in the belly of a fish. This energy and effort to flee the presence of God does not seem to match the efforts put forth to follow God's command. I think this point is often the case, God gives us directions and we go crazy. I believe the problem is we believe that the battle is ours and not God's. We take the assignment personal and we become distracted by the work needed to be done rather than focus on obeying God. Immediately obeying God must be our main priority.

This seems unbelievably easy and Jonah should feel extremely pleased that the people have responded in a way that would be pleasing to God, but not so. This seems like an oxymoron why in the world would this make him angry. I am confused, what about you? There is not a lot of information about Jonah other than how much he had to go through in order to follow the will of God. This study reveals so much about this story that has been made relevant to me over the years. This is really a great example of someone who was in their feelings for whatever reason. Let us keep studying and learning more.

Jonah's Anger and the LORD's Compassion

4 But it displeased Jonah exceedingly,[a] and he was angry. ² And he prayed to the LORD and said, "O LORD, is not this what I said when I was yet in my country? That is why I made haste to flee to Tarshish; for I knew that you are a gracious God and merciful, slow to anger and abounding in steadfast love, and relenting from disaster. ³ Therefore now, O LORD, please take my life from me, for it is better for me to die than to live." ⁴ And the LORD said, "Do you do well to be angry?"

⁵ Jonah went out of the city and sat to the east of the city and made a booth for himself there. He sat under it in the shade, till he should see what would become of the city. ⁶ Now the LORD God appointed a plant[b] and made it come up over Jonah, that it might be a shade over his head, to save him from his discomfort.[c] So Jonah was exceedingly glad because of the plant. ⁷ But when dawn came up the next day, God appointed a worm that attacked the plant, so that it withered. ⁸ When the sun rose, God appointed a scorching east wind, and the sun beat down on the head of Jonah so that he was faint. And he asked that he might die and said, "It is better for me to die than to live." ⁹ But God said to Jonah, "Do you do well to be angry for the plant?" And he said, "Yes, I do well to be angry, angry enough to die." ¹⁰ And the LORD said, "You pity the plant, for which you did not labor, nor did you make it grow, which came into being in a night and perished in a night. ¹¹ And should not I pity

Nineveh, that great city, in which there are more than 120,000 persons who do not know their right hand from their left, and also much cattle?"

Points to Consider: Wow speechless response from Jonah. I do not ever remember anyone ever highlighting this rather bizarre response by him. The response is so bizarre and crazy one would have to wonder how he could respond like this after all that God had done for him. I mean he is angry and wants to die because he is so angry at God's response to the city and the people. The interesting thing is he goes so far to say he flees God's presence because he knew God was gracious and merciful. Let us take another look at what he says.

But it displeased Jonah exceedingly,[a] and he was angry. 2 And he prayed to the Lord and said, "O Lord, is not this what I said when I was yet in my country? That is why I made haste to flee to Tarshish; for I knew that you are a gracious God and merciful, slow to anger and abounding in steadfast love, and relenting from disaster. 3 Therefore now, O Lord, please take my life from me, for it is better for me to die than to live." 4 And the Lord said, "Do you do well to be angry?"

Jonah is big mad; I mean he is furious to the point he prays to God and shares his thoughts to God. Now this part really caught me by surprise. Jonah immediately flees the presence of God when we first meet him, then he was thrown overboard into a raging sea, he is swallowed by a fish, appointed by God to rescue him. He remains in the belly of the fish until he prays. We see he does not pray immediately it takes him three days before he decides to pray. First problem who in their right mind waits that long to reach out to God? He finally does and do what God commands after all this foolishness has taken place. Through all of this we never see where he got angry or wanted to die like he says now. In fact, he does not pray one time although God is showing him extreme mercy all along the way.

So, Jonah has the audacity to pray to God with an attitude because he is big mad that God has shown the people the same mercy, he has shown him time and time again. How dare him? How in the world does he find himself in a place where he is this self-centered and opinionated? He knows and offers his rationale as to why he fled from the presence of God; it makes absolutely no sense, but he offers as if it does. Jonah has been crazy for several reasons: first he goes to God and says I knew you were not going to do anything and that is why I did not want to go. In so many words that is what he is saying in such a petty way.

These are the words of Jonah as to why he decides to flee, "O Lord, is not this what I said when I was yet in my country? That is why I made haste to flee to Tarshish; for I knew that you are a gracious God and merciful, slow to anger and abounding in steadfast love, and relenting from disaster.

Jonah decides to become brave and ignorant at the wrong time. The craziest thing is we are not that far removed from our thinking either. There have been times where we want mercy but we do not want mercy shown to others. I have thought that I am sure you must, but I would not be brave enough to go to God and say how you dare show them mercy. This is basically what he is saying to God in prayer. We know it took him three days to humble himself and pray while in the belly of the fish. This time the conditions are totally different, but yet he goes to God and complains about something that essentially has nothing to do with him, but all to do with God.

The extremely interesting thing here is God goes through enormous lengths to persuade Jonah to follow his directions. We know that Jonah does not follow immediately but he runs away and ends up in the belly of a fish when he finally responds to God's command. The king and all the people repent and turn from their evil ways with little to no persuading unlike Jonah. The king even issues a proclamation over the city and going so far as to say even the beast will be held accountable to the word of the God.

This story is truly remarkable for several reasons that reach far beyond just Jonah being swallowed in the belly of the fish. I pray that you enjoyed learning about him as much as I did. I know I will never look at this story quite the same ever again. My hope is that you as the reader want either. We see he was extremely mad, and he was all up in his feelings. The moral of the story is God shows mercy on whomever he wants to show mercy on. God's purpose will be fulfilled despite your opinion about his purpose. Finally, just obey God and follow his word immediately after he shares it with you. Trust that God knows the beginning and the end of a thing therefore always pray about everything.

CHAPTER 5

HIDDEN INTENTIONS

The next person we will venture out to study and uncover new and surprising discoveries will be Samson. He was one of the judges of Israel. Samson is known for his enormous strength and his love of women. As we read about his life watch closely to see what we can learn not to mock or pock fun at his life but to prevent us repeating his same mistakes. We will discover the bitter feuds between him and his enemy and how often he gets caught up in his feelings. Let us see what amazing information we discover from his life. In this story we find a modern-day hero who gets caught up in his feelings and essentially cost him his life.

Judges 16 New International Version (NIV)

Samson and Delilah

16 One day Samson went to Gaza, where he saw a prostitute. He went in to spend the night with her. [2] The people of Gaza were told, "Samson is here!" So they surrounded the place and lay in wait for him all night at the city gate. They made no move during the night, saying, "At dawn we'll kill him." [3] But Samson lay there only until the middle of the night. Then he got up and took hold of the doors of the city gate, together with the two posts, and tore them loose, bar and all.

He lifted them to his shoulders and carried them to the top of the hill that faces Hebron.

Points to Consider: We see here his love for women and the hatred his enemies had for him. Although he appears to be out of sort, we discover the exact opposite. They plan to attack him at dawn, but he woke up in the middle of the night. I would like to think, in fact it is my belief that God woke him up and directed him as to what to do. I do not believe he just wakes up by happen stance. I believe this incident is very intentional by God. The text does not mention it but knowing how meticulous God is I see him at work here. Besides that, Samson is not at the prostitute's house to pray for her, he is there for a particular purpose and his mind is probably not focused on his enemies if you know what I mean. We see the enemy is already aware of where he is and what he is doing. I do not know why they would wait till morning to attack him. Maybe they figured he would be sound asleep and easier to capture during this time. The trap the enemy set for him does not work and they ended up getting the city doors destroyed and carried off. We see here that trying to capture him was no easy task and many, many more plans will have to be put into place in the attempt to capture him.

[4] Some time later, he fell in love with a woman in the Valley of Sorek whose name was Delilah. [5] The rulers of the Philistines went to her and said, "See if you can lure him into showing you the secret of his great strength and how we can overpower him so we may tie him up and subdue him. Each one of us will give you eleven hundred shekels[a] of silver."[6] So Delilah said to Samson, "Tell me the secret of your great strength and how you can be tied up and subdued."[7] Samson answered her, "If anyone ties me with seven fresh bowstrings that have not been dried, I'll become as weak as any other man."[8] Then the rulers of the Philistines brought her seven fresh bowstrings that had not been dried, and she tied him with them. [9] With men hidden in the room, she called

to him, "Samson, the Philistines are upon you!" But he snapped the bowstrings as easily as a piece of string snaps when it comes close to a flame. So the secret of his strength was not discovered.[10] Then Delilah said to Samson, "You have made a fool of me; you lied to me. Come now, tell me how you can be tied." [11] He said, "If anyone ties me securely with new ropes that have never been used, I'll become as weak as any other man." [12] So Delilah took new ropes and tied him with them. Then, with men hidden in the room, she called to him, "Samson, the Philistines are upon you!" But he snapped the ropes off his arms as if they were threads.[13] Delilah then said to Samson, "All this time you have been making a fool of me and lying to me. Tell me how you can be tied." He replied, "If you weave the seven braids of my head into the fabric on the loom and tighten it with the pin, I'll become as weak as any other man." So while he was sleeping, Delilah took the seven braids of his head, wove them into the fabric [14] and[b] tightened it with the pin. Again she called to him, "Samson, the Philistines are upon you!" He awoke from his sleep and pulled up the pin and the loom, with the fabric.[15] Then she said to him, "How can you say, 'I love you,' when you won't confide in me? This is the third time you have made a fool of me and haven't told me the secret of your great strength." [16] With such nagging she prodded him day after day until he was sick to death of it. [17] So he told her everything. "No razor has ever been used on my head," he said, "because I have been a Nazirite dedicated to God from my mother's womb. If my head were shaved, my strength would leave me, and I would become as weak as any other man."[18] When Delilah saw that he had told her everything, she sent word to the rulers of the Philistines, "Come back once more; he has told me everything." So the rulers of the Philistines returned with the silver in their hands. [19] After putting him to sleep on her lap, she called for someone to shave off the seven braids of his hair, and so began to subdue him.[c] And his strength left him. [20] Then she called, "Samson, the Philistines are upon you!" He awoke from his sleep and thought, "I'll go out as before and shake myself free." But he did not know that the LORD had left him. [21] Then the Philistines seized him, gouged out his eyes and took him down to Gaza. Binding him with bronze shackles, they set him to grinding grain in the prison. [22] But the hair on his head began to grow again after it had been shaved.

Points to Consider: Wow, so we see how a cleaver plan unfolds based on Samson's enemies studying his weakness. Obviously, his enemies have spent countless hours studying Samson and his weakness of women. When the study starts, we see him arriving at a prostitute's house. The bible was noticeably clear on that. When we study his life, we know that he has had some real challenges with frolicking and his sexual craves with foreign women. In studying his life, you learn that his parent encourages him to marry within his race and he out right refuses his parents' request. The refusal is a huge disrespect of his parents, especially during a time where honoring your parents' wishes were extremely important.

Samson moves forward against his parents' wishes and marry someone outside of his tribe and ends up in a disaster. This is just the start of his mishaps with women and it continues to his demise and his enemies took full advantage of this major weakness of his. One would think that he had to be aware of his weakness of women would one day catch up with him, but we see that he does not. This does not mean he does not have his guard up because he does, as we can see in the story we just read. The problem is he had never run into a Delilah before now and she was very persuasive and convincing to the point he falls for her tricks.

My concern is it would appear to me that he would have caught on to her tricks after the first or second time. What is going on with him that he does not know, I am confused. Her intentions seem so obvious to me but why not to him. How in the world does he not recognize what is going on here, especially since she kept on asking and then saying you have made a fool of me? My question is, how can she say, you are making a fool of me? I mean what in the world is he thinking it just seem ludicrous to me. Why does he not ask, how am I making a fool of you when it is just me and you sharing in this matter? The text does not share with us that he is aware of the men lying in wait in the other room to attack him.

The story goes on with her continuing to push and pull on him about his strength. The money had her all twisted up, along with her reputation. Surely the men approached her because they knew that although he was in love with her, she was not in love with him or a least the text shares with us that he is in love but it never states that she is and that is extremely dangerous in any situation, especially this one.

So, she is relentless in her pursuit of finding the answer to his strength here but he is so in love that he does not see it. We can look at this story and see that he was not the first person to have this problem. How many times have we found ourselves in a similar situation or know someone in this same situation?

Let us look at what happens next. she said to him, "How can you say, 'I love you,' when you won't confide in me? This is the third time you have made a fool of me and haven't told me the secret of your great strength." [16] With such nagging she prodded him day after day until he was sick to death of it. [17] So he told her everything. "No razor has ever been used on my head," he said, "because I have been a Nazirite dedicated to God from my mother's womb. If my head were shaved, my strength would leave me, and I would become as weak as any other man."[18] When Delilah saw that he had told her everything, she sent word to the rulers of the Philistines, "Come back once more; he has told me everything."

We see here she simply wore him down with asking the questions about his strength. I would think this would make him very leery of her actions and intentions, but he does not. He never even considers her obvious intentions. She was obviously very clever and persuasive in her interactions because we see she never got discouraged along the way.

I often wondered was it the money she was so in love with or the challenge of being the one who took down God's champion. The Philistines were committed to killing Samson and without her help it was impossible. Interesting we see she has been studying him and his behaviors to the point she recognizes that he is telling the truth, the whole truth and nothing but the truth. The sad thing is that he is obviously so in love with her that he is blinded to what her true intentions are. This is probably the biggest debacle in modern history where a modern-day superhero is taken down by a woman of common physical strength. The woman possesses the power to break down a man of such great physical strength from God all for the love of money.

Although we know there is something far greater at work here with Sampson and the Philistines it is so disheartening to see the fall of such a mighty man of God. We have seen this fall happen repeatedly. The fall is more about the enemy of God (Satan) who goes to and from on the earth seeking whom he may devour. The fall of man is more about attempting to anger God than destroying man. Satan is aware he does not have the power to destroy God or to alter God's plans however he enjoys attempting to show man's weakness exposed before God and the people who are fixed on man's success or lack of success. Since Satan knows the great love that God has for man he seeks to affect or hinder this powerful love God has for man. Let us see what happens to Samson as a result of his enemy now having the upper hand.

The Death of Samson

[23] Now the rulers of the Philistines assembled to offer a great sacrifice to Dagon their god and to celebrate, saying, "Our god has delivered Samson, our enemy, into our hands." [24] When the people saw him, they praised their god, saying, "Our god has delivered our enemy into our

hands, the one who laid waste our land and multiplied our slain."[25] While they were in high spirits, they shouted, "Bring out Samson to entertain us." So they called Samson out of the prison, and he performed for them. When they stood him among the pillars, [26] Samson said to the servant who held his hand, "Put me where I can feel the pillars that support the temple, so that I may lean against them." [27] Now the temple was crowded with men and women; all the rulers of the Philistines were there, and on the roof were about three thousand men and women watching Samson perform. [28] Then Samson prayed to the LORD, "Sovereign LORD, remember me. Please, God, strengthen me just once more, and let me with one blow get revenge on the Philistines for my two eyes." [29] Then Samson reached toward the two central pillars on which the temple stood. Bracing himself against them, his right hand on the one and his left hand on the other, [30] Samson said, "Let me die with the Philistines!" Then he pushed with all his might, and down came the temple on the rulers and all the people in it. Thus he killed many more when he died than while he lived.

[31] Then his brothers and his father's whole family went down to get him. They brought him back and buried him between Zorah and Eshtaol in the tomb of Manoah his father. He had led[d] Israel twenty years

> **Points to Consider:** The underline hidden agenda is now open to everyone and for everyone to see the enemy of God by way of Dagon the Philistine's god. The philistines are feeling great based on their life time achievement of capturing the man of God with his great strength. This has been a long time coming to celebrate the capture and defeat of God's champion. What greater way than to sacrifice the man of God chosen by God than to sacrifice him to this pagan god Dagon? We now see them assembled and boasting about Samson falling from grace and their god delivering him in to their hands.

[23] Now the rulers of the Philistines assembled to offer a great sacrifice to Dagon their god and to celebrate, saying, "Our god has delivered Samson, our enemy, into our hands." [24] When the people saw him, they praised their god, saying, "Our god has delivered our enemy into our hands, the one who laid waste our land and multiplied our slain."[25]

Samson did not have to die, he chose to die. Samson could have asked for a way of escape, but he chose not to out of his frustrations. This lets us know that we can't allow the enemy to frustrate us because if so we choose death over life.

CHAPTER 6

NEVER UNDERESTIMATE THE COURAGE OF A BOY

This next person we shall study I must admit he is one of my favorite persons in the bible. I really admire his dedication and commitment to God. He is the only man God said is the apple of my eye. He won many battles both on the field and off the field. Here is where we first see young David as a boy instructed by his father Jessie to take some lunch to his three older brothers. This is a remarkably interesting point of his life where we see David's commitment to carry out his father's directions to specificity. I believe this allows us to see the type of father and king he will be. This story is going to take many twists and turns but it will be epic. The story begins talking about the fierce battle between Israel and the Philistines. So, let us go to work.

Choose a man for yourselves, and let him come down to me. ²If he is able to fight with me and strike me down, we will then become your servants. But if I prevail against him and strike him down, you will become our servants and serve us." ¹⁰The Phi·lis′tine then said: "I do taunt* the battle line of Israel̲ this day. Give me a man, and let us fight it out!" ¹¹When Saul and all Israel heard these words of the Phi·lis′tine, they became terrified and greatly afraid. ¹²Now David was the son of the Eph′rath·ite̲m from Beth′le·hem̲n of Judah named Jes′se̲,o who had eight sons_p and who in the days of Saul was already an old man. [13] The three oldest sons of Jes'se had followed Saul to the war._q The names of his three sons who went to war were E·li'ab_r the firstborn, his second son A·bin'a·dab,_s and the third Sham'mah.t [14] David was the youngest,_u and the three oldest followed Saul. [15] David was going back and forth from Saul to tend the sheep_v of his father at Beth'le·hem. [16] Meanwhile, the Phi·lis'tine would come forward and take his position each morning and each evening for 40 days.

Points to Consider: We see here where the Philistines have offered a solution as to how to end the fighting. Their idea was that both armies will select a warrior and the winner of that battle will be the group that the loosing team will follow. This sounds like a great idea; however, you must ask yourself why were they so willing to bet everything on one fighter. We know that Israel has a good record for winning battles because God was with them. So, it makes sense to try and fight two men rather than thousands of men. This limits the opportunity for men being slaughtered in battle. However, we discover they have a secret weapon in their midst. They have a huge giant in their camp. The giant is so large that no man is brave enough to take on this giant and battle him. We discover that this taunting has been going on for a while and no man in Israel is willing to step up and battle this giant name Goliath. They hear him calling them out every day but so for no one is willing to step up and take on this giant. I do recognize and understand that the giant was extremely large but surely you would think there was at least one champion in Israel to step up and take on this giant.

[17] Then Jes'se said to his son David: "Take, please, this e'phah* of roasted grain and these ten loaves of bread, and carry them quickly to your brothers in the camp. [18] And take these ten portions of cheese* to the chief of the thousand; also, you should check on the welfare of your brothers and bring back some token from them." [19] They were with

Saul and all the other men of Israel in the Valley* of E'lah,w fighting against the Phi·lis'tines.x ²⁰So David got up early in the morning and left someone in charge of the sheep; then he packed up and went just as Jes'se had commanded him. When he came to the camp enclosure, the army was going out to the battle line, shouting a battle cry. ²¹Israel and the Phi·lis'tines drew up so that one battle line faced the other battle line. ²²David immediately left his baggage in the care of the baggage keeper and ran to the battle line. When he arrived, he began asking about the welfare of his brothers.y ²³While he was speaking with them, there came the champion named Go·li'ath,z the Phi·lis'tine from Gath. He came out from the battle line of the Phi·lis'tines, and he spoke the same words as before,a and David heard him. ²⁴When all the men of Israel saw the man, they fled from him, terrified.b

Points to Consider: We see David following the instructions of his father with earnest conviction. We know this because he wakes up early in the morning to do exactly as his father Jessie has asked of him. We also see David does not just leave without ensuring someone would oversee his father's sheep. This shows his keenness to his responsibility to what he has been charged to do by his father. David does not neglect his responsibility to his assignment even though his father has given him a task to do concerning his brothers' welfare during their time at war with King Saul. David's father distinctly commands David to take his brothers some food and check on their wellbeing.

David arrives just in time as the troops are headed out for battle that morning. He immediately leaves his baggage in the care of the baggage keeper and ran to the battle line and immediately asked about the welfare of his brothers. This again shows David's keen awareness of taking care of his responsibilities despite his current dynamic. David does not just drop everything and run to see about his brothers, he drops off his baggage to the baggage keeper for safe keeping. This shows us that David is a very responsible young man. We do not see him getting excited about what is going on to the point that he forgets his responsibilities. The text shows him not leaving the sheep unattended or dropping the bags and running to the battle lines simply because he arrives at a time the soldiers are heading to the battle lines or because his father has given him a new task. We see David as a responsible young boy who carries out his instructions from his father with fidelity. What we do not see is a young ill responsible young boy who is easily distracted. David shows remarkable signs of being able to stay on course despite the circumstances surrounding him. This is an especially important observation, that at an incredibly early age he has the capacity to remain focused and on task.

[25] The men of Israel were saying: "Have you seen this man who is coming out? He comes to taunt* Israel.c The king will give great riches to the man who strikes him down, he will give him his own daughter,d and he will give the house of his father exemption in Israel." [26] David began to say to the men who were standing near him: "What will be done for the man who strikes down that Phi·lis′tine over there and takes away reproach from Israel? For who is this uncircumcised Phi·lis′tine that he should taunt* the battle line of the living God?"e [27] Then the people told him the same thing as before: "This is what will be done for the man who strikes him down." [28] When his oldest brother E·li′abf heard him speak to the men, he became angry with David and said: "Why have you come down? And with whom did you leave those few sheep in the wilderness?g I well know your presumptuousness and the bad intentions of your heart; you came down just to see the battle." [29] To this David said: "What have I done now? I was only asking a question!" [30] So he turned from him toward someone else and asked the same thing as before,h and the people gave him the same reply as before.i [31] The words that David had spoken were overheard and reported to Saul. So he sent for him. [32] David said to Saul: "Let no one lose heart* because of him. Your servant will go and fight with this Phi·lis′tine."j [33] But Saul said to

David: "You are not able to go fight against this Phi·lis'tine, for you are but a boy,k and he has been a soldier* from his youth." 34 David then said to Saul: "Your servant became a shepherd of his father's flock, and a lionl came, also a bear, and each carried off a sheep from the flock. 35 I went out after it and struck it down and rescued it from its mouth. When it rose up against me, I grabbed it by its fur* and struck it down and put it to death. 36 Your servant struck down both the lion and the bear, and this uncircumcised Phi·lis'tine will become like one of them, for he has taunted* the battle lines of the living God."m 37 Then David added: "Jehovah, who rescued me from the claws of the lion and the bear, he is the one who will rescue me from the hand of this Phi·lis'tine."n At this Saul said to David: "Go, and may Jehovah be with you.

Points to Consider: We make a special note here that David hears someone from the enemy's camp saying all manner of foul things against the Israelites and their God. David notices that no one is addressing this giant and when he approaches them, they flee and tremble with fear. David inquires of his brothers as his father has instructed him to do so however in doing so it is obvious that the men are terrified and running in fear. The King James translation of the **Bible** reports the **giant** Goliath as "six cubits and a span" in **height**—about nine feet nine inches tall.

So, we see here David having conversations with the soldiers. The soldiers are explaining to David how the Philistine giant has been coming out every morning taunting them and asking for a challenger to fight him; however no one is brave enough to take on the giant. The giant Goliath size alone made men tremble with fear. We note here that the men were so afraid when he came out to the battle lines that the men ran. I am sure Goliath and the Philistine armies enjoyed seeing this happen. The question I have always wondered was, why not just attack the Israelites and over take them? Seems like this would be a no brainer and an extremely easy victory for them. Well, they were no fools they knew very well the reputation that the God of Israel had on defeating the armies of their enemies. So, the strategy seems simple here, let us scare them into submission and we have an easy victory.

In David's conversation with the men, he discovers that the King has put up a reward in order to encourage a champion of Israel to come forward to fight this giant. The men were terrified even though King Saul had put up his daughter as a prize to the winner and his family would be free of taxes. While David is inquiring about this information out of nowhere his older brothers show up and began to taut him as thought to discredit him and make him feel less than. I thought this was very bizarre for several reasons. First reason is these are David's brothers to whom he was there to bring food and to check on their safety for their father. When his oldest brother E·li'ab heard him speak to the men, he became angry with David and said: "Why have you come down? And with whom did you leave those few sheep in the wilderness? I well know your presumptuousness and the bad intentions of your heart; you came down just to see the battle." To this David said: "What have I done now? I was only asking a question!" So, he turned from him toward someone else and asked the same thing as before.

Why does his own brothers try to joke him and belittle him, of all people? This points out that there are times where the people you think should be in your corner are not. Although he comes to bring them food, we see his older brother question him like where are those few sheep you are supposed to be watching. This attitude is totally out of line especially now; however, there is one especially important thing we must consider here. This is David's older brother, and the text tells us he becomes angry. The scripture does not tell us why he becomes angry. I believe he becomes angry because he realizes that his litter brother now recognizes that his older brother who he should be looking up to because of his bravery is afraid also. I mean why else would he instantly become angry at his little brother for asking questions and talking other than him getting into his feelings. Eliab's pride causes him to lash out at David. Think about it like this. Eliab knows very well that David is obligated to report back to their father Jessie the statues of his sons. I can imagine as the older brother he towered over David in size before the war he appeared to be very brave. Out of fear he realizes that David will report this back to their father, so he wanted to belittle David and distract him from finding out what was happening to prevent him from reporting back to their father the acts of cowardliness. I believe that this was just an attempt to distract David however we see that is a custom to him trying to belittle him, but David does not allow him to distract him. To this David said: "What have I done now? I was only asking a question!" So, he turned from him toward someone else and asked the same thing as before and the people gave him the same reply as before. The words that David had spoken were overheard and reported to Saul.

David is looking at a much bigger picture than the big brother who is in his feelings about the news that David will need to take back to their father. In fact, what David is looking to do will set the entire family up for life? David wants to know what will become of the man who kills the Philistine giant and David wants to be sure. The men immediately recognize what his own brothers do not and that's David's unwavering bravery. Now we see this news gets back to the King. The king is looking for a champion so of course this is great news to report to the king. I am sure this is the best news the king has gotten in an exceptionally long time.

So, we learn here, the words that David had spoken were overheard and reported to Saul. So, he sent for him. I would imagine this conversation would be led and dominated by the King, however it is the exact opposite. David said to Saul: "Let no one lose heart because of him. Your servant will go and fight with this Philistine." This powerful and bold statement probably made king Saul's heart drop. I am sure he was confident that he had recruited the biggest and strongest men that Israel had to offer in all the land. To see this little boy, show up out of nowhere and to talk with such confidence I see why King Saul is not talking in amazement at this point. I am sure when he heard of David's confidence, he was extremely happy but seeing him in person and recognizing his size and stature there was some disbelief and great concern in the king's heart and mind, but we see David speaking with authority and boldness in the presence of the king.

But Saul said to David: "You are not able to go fight against this Philistine, for you are but a boy, and he has been a soldier from his youth." Saul quickly realizes that perhaps his hopes has gotten too high. He sees David with a natural eye like we sometimes see each other rather than from our spiritual eyes. Saul in disbelief tries to explain to a confident David that Goliath has been fighting since his youth and now he is a full-grown man. I can imagine Saul saying boy this man will crush you like nothing. What we see here is God taking foolish things to confine the wise. Everyone knows that without supernatural help David won't to survive this battle. David yet again remains focused and unmoved by what the king is saying about Goliath.

After hearing King Saul run down Goliath's resume' David gave his testimony. David then said to Saul: "Your servant became a shepherd of his father's flock, and a lion came, also a bear, and each carried off a sheep from the flock. I went out after it and struck it down and rescued it from it's mouth. When it revolted against me, I grabbed it by its fur and struck it down and put it to death. Your servant struck down both the lion and the bear, and this uncircumcised Philistine will become like one of them, for he has taunted the battle lines of the living God." Then David added: "Jehovah, who rescued me from the claws of the lion and the bear, he is the one who will rescue me from the hand of this Philistine." At this Saul said to David: "Go, and may Jehovah be with you.

David explains that this victory is not mine, it is the Lord's, and God did it before he will do it again. To this Saul's only response is Jehovah be with you. Saul has enough wisdom to recognize that if God is with him then so am I.

"<u>38</u> Saul now clothed David with his garments. He put a copper helmet on his head, after which he clothed him with a coat of mail. <u>39</u> Then David strapped on his sword over his garments and tried to go but could not, for he was not used to them. David said to Saul: "I am unable to go in these things, for I am not used to them." So David took them off. <u>40</u> He then took his staff in his hand and chose five smooth stones from the streambed<u>*</u> and placed them in the pouch of his shepherd's bag, and his sling<u>o</u> was in his hand. And he began approaching the Phi·lis'tine. <u>41</u> The Phi·lis'tine came closer and closer to David, and his shield-bearer was ahead of him. <u>42</u> When the Phi·lis'tine looked and saw David, he sneered at him in contempt because he was just a ruddy and handsome boy.<u>p</u> <u>43</u> So the Phi·lis'tine said to David: "Am I a dog,<u>q</u> so that you are coming against me with sticks?" With that the Phi·lis'tine cursed David by his gods. <u>44</u> The Phi·lis'tine said to David: "Just come to me, and I will give your flesh to the birds of the heavens and to the beasts of the field." <u>45</u> David replied to the Phi·lis'tine: "You are coming against me with sword and spear and javelin,<u>r</u> but I am coming against you in the name of Jehovah of armies,<u>s</u> the God of the battle line of Israel, whom you have taunted.<u>*t</u> <u>46</u> This very day Jehovah will surrender you into my hand,<u>u</u> and I will strike you down and cut off your head; and on this day I will give the corpses of the camp of the Phi·lis'tines to the birds of the heavens and to the wild beasts of the earth; and people of all the earth will know that there is a God in Israel.<u>v</u> <u>47</u> And all those gathered here<u>*</u> will know that it is not with the sword or the spear that Jehovah saves,<u>w</u> for the battle belongs to Jehovah,<u>x</u> and he will give all of you into our hand."<u>y</u> <u>48</u> Then the Phi·lis'tine rose and drew steadily closer to meet David, but David ran quickly toward the battle line to meet the Phi·lis'tine. <u>49</u> David thrust his hand into his bag and took a stone from there and slung it. He struck the Phi·lis'tine in the forehead, and the stone sank into his forehead and he fell facedown on the ground.z ⁵⁰ So David prevailed over the Phi·lis′tine with a sling and a stone; he struck down the Phi·lis′tine and put him to death, though there was no sword in David's hand.a ⁵¹ David continued running and stood over him. Then he took hold of the Phi·lis′tine's swordb and pulled it out of its sheath and made sure that he was dead by cutting off his head with it. When the Phi·lis′tines saw that their mighty one had died, they fled.c ⁵² At that the men of Israel and of Judah rose and broke into shouting and pursued the Phi·lis′tines all the way from the valleyd to the gates of Ek′ron,e and the slain of the Phi·lis′tines lay fallen along the road from Sha′a·ra′im,f as far as Gath and Ek′ron. ⁵³ After the Israelites returned from hotly pursuing the Phi·lis′tines, they pillaged their camps. ⁵⁴ Then David took the head of the Phi·lis′tine and brought it to Jerusalem, but he put the Phi·lis′tine's weapons in his own tent.g

Points to Consider: What do we learn from this? One we see that we cannot always fight with another man's armor, it may work one time or another but it is important to use the armor of the Lord. When we allow the armor that God provides for us, we are sure to experience victory. I am reminded that weapons of our warfare are not carnal but spiritual. David recognizes this immediately although God allowed David to win the other two victories using his hands this time, we see God using something totally outside of anyone's belief that would work. There are a few interesting things to point out here, for one David did not come to the battle to fight. The opportunity presents itself because of what David over hears. David recognizes that it is not okay to speak against God or the armies of God. This apparently did not bother anyone but David for some reason. Perhaps out of fear everyone even the king was too afraid to address this behavior.

David takes a huge stance from the moment he arrives on the scene. David uses wisdom and diplomacy with the soldiers and the king. David does not go off on the soldiers or his brothers for being cowards. David listens and quickly decides to do something about this injustice being done against God. A decision any listener who loves God could have and should have made. What we see here is David's relationship toward God even as a young boy is incredibly strong. Strong enough where he refuses to let this manner of conversation continue in his presence and even though he did not come to fight he is prepared to fight for his God. David is willing to fight whereas none of the so-called brave soldiers at the battle are willing to take on the champion.

Saul tries his best to help by giving David his armor. We know that the king had the best armor, but his armor was no good to David. The armor did not fit for David was just a boy and King Saul was a full-grown man. This was not a setback for David because his trust was not in man but in his God. David never lost confidence in God no matter what was going on around him. We see fear in the camp all around him and we see the king has not been able to find anyone to fight Goliath and now you have young David who quickly accepts the challenge to defend God.

David takes the challenge that no other soldier or man has been brave enough to do. David did not come prepared to fight however despite not coming to the battle to fight, he refuses to standby and listen to this giant talk foolishly about the God he serves. When the Philistines looked and saw David, he sneered at him in contempt because he was just a ruddy and handsome boy. So, the Philistine said to David: "Am I a dog, so that you are coming against me with sticks?" With that the Philistine cursed David by his gods. The Philistine said to David: "Just come to me, and I will give your flesh to the birds of the heavens and to the beasts of the field." David replied to the Philistine: "You are coming against me with sword and spear and javelin, but I am coming against you in the name of Jehovah of armies, the God of the battle line of Israel, whom you have taunted. This very day Jehovah will surrender you into my hand, and I will strike you down and cut off your head; and on this day I will give the corpse of the camp of the Philistines to the birds of the heavens and to the wild beasts of the earth; and people of all the earth will know that there is a God in Israel. The story ends with David's great victory over Goliath and this starts his complicated journey to become one of the greatest Kings of Israel and titled a man after God's own heart. No other man has ever achieved such a statue.

Distractions that lead unto death

Distractions have been and always will be a common part of life. Often time's distractions are so powerful that we cannot get around them no matter how hard we try. In this story we find the king letting down his guard and rather than going off to war he decides he will remain at home. Perhaps he felt he needed a vacation and now is the perfect time to schedule a little R and R rest and relaxation. For all intenseness purposes one would agree that David needed some time to relax from being at war and who could fault him for wanting a little time alone.

David and Bathsheba

11 *ʰⁱ*In the spring of the year, the time when kings go out to battle, David sent Joab, and his servants with him, and all Israel. And they ravaged the Ammonites and besieged *ʲ*Rabbah. But David remained at Jerusalem.

---

² It happened, late one afternoon, when David arose from his couch and was walking on ᵏthe roof of the king's house, that he saw from the roof a woman bathing; and the woman was very beautiful. ³ And David sent and inquired about the woman. And one said, "Is not this ˡBathsheba, the daughter of Eliam, the wife of ᵐUriah the Hittite?" ⁴ So David sent messengers and took her, and she came to him, and he lay with her. (ⁿNow she had been purifying herself from her uncleanness.) Then she returned to her house. ⁵ And the woman conceived, and she sent and told David, "I am pregnant."

Points to Consider: We see here David appears to be either overly rested or unable to rest. This could be because he is accustomed to being out on the battle field at war during this time or he could be tired of resting and became restless sitting around the palace. We see him getting off his couch and going for a walk and walking on the roof. I often wonder why he was walking on the roof top this appears to be a very odd place for the king to be walking. Perhaps he was bored and hoping to find some adventure. Whatever the reason he was on the roof top we know that he saw something he probably would have never seen, one if he was at war like he was supposed to be and two if he was not walking on the roof top. Walking on the roof top gave him a hugely different vantage point or view point to see things that most would not normally see. Perhaps this advantage is his greatest that sets in motion David's greatest down fall. We are getting ready to be introduced to the side of David that we have not been yet exposed to. This side of David comes as a result of not being where he was supposed to be, which was at war and then seeing something he knew that he should not have, but his lust of his eyes took complete advantage of who God was creating him to be.

⁶ So David sent word to Joab, "Send me Uriah the Hittite." And Joab sent Uriah to David. ⁷ When Uriah came to him, David asked how Joab was

doing and how the people were doing and how the war was going. ⁸ Then David said to Uriah, "Go down to your house and ᵃwash your feet." And Uriah went out of the king's house, and there followed him a present from the king. ⁹ But Uriah slept at the door of the king's house with all the servants of his lord, and did not go down to his house. ¹⁰ When they told David, "Uriah did not go down to his house," David said to Uriah, "Have you not come from a journey? Why did you not go down to your house?" ¹¹ Uriah said to David, ᵖ"The ark and Israel and Judah dwell in booths, and my lord Joab and ᵠthe servants of my lord are camping in the open field. Shall I then go to my house, to eat and to drink and to lie with my wife? As you live, and ʳas your soul lives, I will not do this thing." ¹² Then David said to Uriah, "Remain here today also, and tomorrow I will send you back." So Uriah remained in Jerusalem that day and the next. ¹³ And David invited him, and he ate in his presence and drank, ˢso that he made him drunk. And in the evening he went out to lie on his couch with ᵠthe servants of his lord, but he did not go down to his house.

¹⁴ In the morning David ᵗwrote a letter to Joab and sent it by the hand of Uriah. ¹⁵ In the letter he wrote, "Set Uriah in the forefront of the hardest fighting, and then draw back from him, ᵘthat he may be struck down, and die." ¹⁶ And as Joab was besieging the city, he assigned Uriah to the place where he knew there were valiant men. ¹⁷ And the men of the city came out and fought with Joab, and some of the servants of David among the people fell. Uriah the Hittite also died. ¹⁸ Then Joab sent and told David all the news about the fighting. ¹⁹ And he instructed the messenger, "When you have finished telling all the news about the fighting to the king, ²⁰ then, if the king's anger rises, and if he says to you, 'Why did you go so near the city to fight? Did you not know that they would shoot from the wall? ²¹ ᵛWho killed Abimelech the son of Jerubbesheth? Did not a woman cast an upper millstone on him from

the wall, so that he died at Thebez? Why did you go so near the wall?' then you shall say, 'Your servant Uriah the Hittite is dead also.' "

²² So the messenger went and came and told David all that Joab had sent him to tell. ²³ The messenger said to David, "The men gained an advantage over us and came out against us in the field, but we drove them back to the entrance of the gate. ²⁴ Then the archers shot at your servants from the wall. Some of the king's servants are dead, and your servant Uriah the Hittite is dead also." ²⁵ David said to the messenger, "Thus shall you say to Joab, 'Do not let this matter displease you, for the sword devours now one and now another. Strengthen your attack against the city and overthrow it.' And encourage him."

²⁶ When the wife of Uriah heard that Uriah her husband was dead, she lamented over her husband. ²⁷ And when the mourning was over, David sent and brought her to his house, and ʷshe became his wife and bore him a son. But the thing that David had done displeased the LORD.

Nathan Rebukes David

12 And the LORD sent ˣNathan to David. He came to him and said to him, ʸ"There were two men in a certain city, the one rich and the other poor. ² The rich man had very many flocks and herds, ³ but the poor man had nothing but one little ewe lamb, which he had bought. And he brought it up, and it grew up with him and with his children. It used to eat of his morsel and drink from his cup and lie in his arms,ᶻ and it was like a daughter to him. ⁴ Now there came a traveler to the rich man, and he was unwilling to take one of his own flock or herd to prepare for the guest who had come to him, but he took the poor man's lamb and prepared it for the man who had come to him." ⁵ Then David's anger was greatly kindled against the man, and he said to Nathan, ᵃ"As the LORD lives, the man who has done this deserves to die, ⁶ and he shall

restore the lamb ᵃfourfold, because he did this thing, and because he had no pity."

⁷Nathan said to David, "You are the man! Thus says the LORD, the God of Israel, ᵇ'I anointed you king over Israel, and I delivered you out of the hand of Saul. ⁸ And I gave you your master's house and your master's wives into your arms and gave you the house of Israel and of Judah. And if this were too little, I would add to you as much more. ⁹ᶜWhy have you despised the word of the LORD, ᵈto do what is evil in his sight? ᵉYou have struck down Uriah the Hittite with the sword and ᶠhave taken his wife to be your wife and have killed him with the sword of the Ammonites. ¹⁰ Now therefore the sword shall never depart from your house, because you have despised me and have taken the wife of Uriah the Hittite to be your wife.' ¹¹ Thus says the LORD, 'Behold, I will raise up evil against you out of your own house. And I will take your wives before your eyes and give them to your neighbor, and he shall lie with your wives in the sight of this sun. ¹² For you did it secretly, ᵍbut I will do this thing before all Israel and before the sun.' " ¹³ ʰDavid said to Nathan, ⁱ"I have sinned against the LORD." And Nathan said to David, ʲ"The LORD also has put away your sin; you shall not die. ¹⁴ Nevertheless, because by this deed you have utterly ᵏscorned the LORD,² the child who is born to you shall die." ¹⁵ Then Nathan went to his house.

David's Child Dies

And the LORD afflicted the child that Uriah's wife bore to David, and he became sick. ¹⁶ David therefore sought God on behalf of the child. And David ˡfasted and went in ᵐand lay all night on the ground. ¹⁷ And the elders of his house stood beside him, to raise him from the ground, but he would not, nor did he eat food with them. ¹⁸ On the seventh day the child died. And the servants of David were afraid to tell him that the child was dead, for they said, "Behold, while the child was yet alive, we spoke to him, and he did not listen to us. How then can we say to him the child is dead? He may do himself some harm." [19] But when David saw that his servants were whispering together, David understood that the child was dead. And David said to his servants, "Is the child dead?" They said, "He is dead." [20] Then David arose from the earth [n]and washed and anointed himself and changed his clothes. And he went into the house of the LORD [o]and worshiped. He then went to his own house. And when he asked, they set food before him, and he ate. [21] Then his servants said to him, "What is this thing that you have done? You fasted and wept for the child while he was alive; but when the child died, you arose and ate food." [22] He said, "While the child was still alive, I fasted and wept, for I said, [p]'Who knows whether the LORD will be gracious to me, that the child may live?' [23] But now he is dead. Why should I fast? Can I bring him back again? I shall go to him, [q]but he will not return to me."

Points to Consider: So, we see the prophets has come to his house and made him fully aware of his wicked deed before God. David pronounces death to the man who has committed such deeds. Once David realizes that the deeds were his own. God does spare his life; however, there are several consequences to his actions. God states that the sword will never leave David's house.

Now that you have read about the wicked deeds that David has created to cover his sins in the sight of both man and God, there are great consequence's that comes as a result of his actions. The unfortunate thing is that although David sets plans in motion to have Uriah killed, he shows great loyalty to his king and his country. Uriah annihilates David's plan from the onset. I can only imagine David's frustration to Uriah's response to his brilliant plan. For all intense purposes, the plan was surprisingly good and I am sure David was greatly confident in his plan until Uriah goes completely against it. Uriah shows great loyalty to the king and I can only imagine it was like hot coals being place on David's forehead knowing that his plan was not working out. We do not know much about Uriah, but this small example shows his courage, his dedication to his king, and his country. One would have to believe that he had divine intervention, or he was just an upstanding soldier. I mean he went totally against what King David had commanded him to do. In most cases this could be considered treasons; however, Uriah was so dedicated to his belief that he risked treason and sacrificed the comfort of his wife and home to sleep at the king's gates.

When we look at this story, we see so many things taking place here. We see one man's life taken way too soon and without any just cause he was murdered. In addition we see King David's life take a spiritual spiral that will impact the life of him and his children forever. This one incident caused so much chaos as we began to look into this journey of David's life. We will see the chaos unfold and the tragic knife that God spoke of implode in the life of David's family.

CHAPTER 7

WHAT HAPPENS WHEN BLENDED FAMILIES DO NOT BLEND WELL?

Amnon and Tamar

13 Now ^wAbsalom, David's son, had a beautiful sister, whose name was ^xTamar. And after a time Amnon, David's son, loved her. ² And Amnon was so tormented that he made himself ill because of his sister Tamar, for she was a virgin, and it seemed impossible to Amnon to do anything to her. ³ But Amnon had a friend, whose name was Jonadab, the son of ^yShimeah, David's brother. And Jonadab was a very crafty man. ⁴ And he said to him, "O son of the king, why are you so haggard morning after morning? Will you not tell me?" Amnon said to him, "I love Tamar, my brother Absalom's sister." ⁵ Jonadab said to him, "Lie down on your bed and pretend to be ill. And when your father comes to see you, say to him, 'Let my sister Tamar come and give me bread to eat, and prepare the food in my sight, that I may see it and eat it from her hand.' " ⁶ So Amnon lay down and pretended to be ill. And when the king came to see him, Amnon said to the king, "Please let my sister Tamar come and ^zmake a couple of cakes in my sight, that I may eat from her hand."

Points to Consider: Remember God has decreed that the sword will forever be in David's house. So, what exactly does this means? This means that David's whole house is in trouble for a terrible and wick plot that David has planned. This not only impacts David individually, but it impacts David's house just as God has pronounced it.

Now we have a blended household. Blended families do not always work out the way they are expected to. There are times where two people come together and merge their families for the greater good of the family in this case David, being the king of Israel. We know that kings had several wives and several kids for those wives. There are times when the families are blended this way, we discover that feelings can and often do develop from siblings who may not necessarily share moms and dads together. When this happens, there is a since of connection that cannot be controlled. This connection can be taken in the positive or the negative. The spiritual connection shows a positive connection as a result of the parents DNA and should be developed in a way that the entire family benefits from it. Then there are times where the connection is so strong and misconstrued on the negative end and taken out of proportion. We see here a half-brother who has fallen head over hills in love with his sister. He is so in love with her that he is tormented and now he is plotting to get next to her and on top of that he has help from his friend who just happens to be his first cousin to develop this plan.

The family dynamic appears to be rather jaded even more now seeing that this brother is in love with his sister and he and his cousin plots together to make this happen. Now we see him bring his father David into the plan. In my opinion I believe he is playing on the soft side of his father who believes that he is sick. Because David believes he is sick he is compelled to ask his daughter who is totally innocent in this whole plot to come to her brother's room and do all that he has requested. David has no clue to the plot he has planned for his sister Tamar.

[7] Then David sent home to Tamar, saying, "Go to your brother Amnon's house and prepare food for him." [8] So Tamar went to her brother Amnon's

house, where he was lying down. And she took dough and kneaded it and made cakes in his sight and baked the cakes. [9] And she took the pan and emptied it out before him, but he refused to eat. And Amnon said, [a]"Send out everyone from me." So everyone went out from him. [10] Then Amnon said to Tamar, "Bring the food into the chamber, that I may eat from your hand." And Tamar took the cakes she had made and brought them into the chamber to Amnon her brother. [11] But when she brought them near him to eat, he took hold of her and said to her, "Come, lie with me, my sister." [12] She answered him, "No, my brother, do not violate[l] me, for [b]such a thing is not done in Israel; do not do this [c]outrageous thing. [13] As for me, where could I carry my shame? And as for you, you would be as one of [d]the outrageous fools in Israel. Now therefore, please speak to the king, for he will not withhold me from you." [14] But he would not listen to her, and being stronger than she, he violated her and lay with her.

Points to Consider: Wow, I can imagine Amnon who was in love with his sister really enjoyed watching his sister prepare his meal. In all his lust filled greed for her he probably really got off on watching her make this meal for him however this was not enough for him. I would like to think he was looking to violate her at first but watching her has sent him into even more of a rage where he must have her now. He was already taken by her and by watching her has caused even more lust to build up inside of him.

We see that he refuses to eat and now he sends everyone out of the room and ask her to feed him and like an innocent sister she does as her brother has requested. Once everyone left out of the room, he decides to have his way with her but before he does, he at least asks her to sleep with him. What she says next is amazing. "No, my brother, do not violate me, for such a thing is not done in Israel; do not do this outrageous thing. As for me, where could I carry my shame? And as for you, you would be as one of the outrageous fools in Israel. Now therefore, please speak to the king, for he will not withhold me from you." [14] But he would not listen to her, and being stronger than she, he violated her and lay with her.

She tries to convince her brother, but he would not listen to her she even states that if he really wants her, all he must do is ask the king and the king will give her to him. None of this logic made any sense to him. He acts in complete rage and out of control while his lust takes over him and he simply wanted what he wanted and that was to rape her. The so-called love has now caused him to violate her innocence.

[15] Then Amnon hated her with very great hatred, so that the hatred with which he hated her was greater than the love with which he had loved her. And Amnon said to her, "Get up! Go!" [16] But she said to him, "No, my brother, for this wrong in sending me away is greater than the other that you did to me."[2] But he would not listen to her. [17] He called the young man who served him and said, "Put this woman out of my presence and bolt the door after her." [18] Now she was wearing [e]a long robe with sleeves, [f] for thus were the virgin daughters of the king dressed. So, his servant put her out and bolted the door after her. [19] And Tamar [f]put ashes on her head and [g]tore the long robe that she wore. And [h]she laid her hand on her head and went away, crying aloud as she went.

[20] And her brother Absalom said to her, "Has Amnon your brother been with you? Now hold your peace, my sister. He is your brother; do not take this to heart." So Tamar lived, a desolate woman, in her brother Absalom's house. [21] When King David heard of all these things, he was very angry.[i] [22] But Absalom spoke to Amnon [j]neither good nor bad, for Absalom hated Amnon, because he had violated his sister Tamar.

Absalom Murders Amnon

[23] After two full years Absalom had *sheep shearers at Baal-hazor, which is near Ephraim, and Absalom invited all the king's sons. [24] And Absalom came to the king and said, "Behold, your servant has sheepshearers. Please let the king and his servants go with your servant." [25] But the king said to Absalom, "No, my son, let us not all go, lest we be burdensome to you." He pressed him, but he would not go but gave him his blessing. [26] Then Absalom said, "If not, please let my brother Amnon go with us." And the king said to him, "Why should he go with you?" [27] But Absalom pressed him until he let Amnon and all the king's sons go with him. [28] Then Absalom commanded his servants, "Mark when Amnon's *heart is merry with wine, and when I say to you, 'Strike Amnon,' then kill him. Do not fear; have I not commanded you? Be courageous and be valiant." [29] So the servants of Absalom did to Amnon as Absalom had commanded. Then all the king's sons arose, and each mounted his mule and fled.

Points to Consider: We see here Absalom, Tamar's brother, is terribly angry at what his half-brother has done to his sister. I am sure the trauma of knowing his half-brother has raped his sister is not something anyone can easily get over. More so than this he consoles his sister, and she lives with him. This allows him to see all the emotional turmoil she has had to endure. We recognized that she understood the degradation of being a defiled Virgin and just wanted her brother to do right by her. This doing right by her would have been to ask her father for her hand in marriage which she reminds him before he rapes her, but he refused to listen.

Now imagine the trauma of the one who has raped you being your half-brother (someone you must meet) repeatedly, perhaps daily. These experiences had to been played out at home before her brother's very eyes. Especially the shame and guilt of no longer being considered pure as a virgin. On top of that she had no control over what happened. I can feel her level of pain and frustration of now being less than who you knew you were created to be. I'm sure Absalom was a supported brother who has firsthand experience of witnessing the hurt and shame his innocent sister has had to experience at the hands of their half-brother. The anger is so great that it has lasted for up to and possible over two years. This gives merit to the degree or level of disenchantment he feels towards his brother. I often wonder does their father David ever pick up on this wedge between his two sons or is he too busy doing other things. What we do know is that David is directly involved and, in a position, where he could potentially make a difference in the outcomes.

During this time, I'm sure Absalom has plotted over and over in his mind how can I revenge my sister? Absalom probably could have used some support from a supportive father. I am not sure what David has done in response to his daughter's experience with her half-brother. What we do know is Absalom plots to revenge his sister by killing his brother. We also know that just like the rape incident their father, David, who is unable to see the destruction before it happens yet again. I believe this is an extremely low point in life where David has the power to change the outcomes but has no clue about where his kids are emotionally or spiritually at this point.

In addition, I like to pinpoint that Amnon was very disrespectful towards his sister and the love he once had for Tamar turned into an even stronger hatred towards her. I am sure like the outward recognition of his love being shown that equally the hatred towards his sister is now being shown as well. I only mention this because the scripture teaches us that he hated her now with an even greater energy than the love he once had for her.

This is a direct result of the father's sins affecting his children. Remember God's punishment for David's murder of an innocent man to take his wife. We see David at both critical moments to actually intervene. The question you must ask is how these two very important tragedies got by David. We see earlier in the book how God shares with Abram what his intentions are about the city his nephew Lot and his family lives in. God sharing his intentions saves Lot and his two daughters lives. The scripture teaches us that warning comes before destruction. In this situation it was already prophesied that the sword would be in David's house and we see it manifested. The other question you must ask your self is what about the spirit of discernment? There are so many questions that you can ask yourself about this situation however it comes down to relationships with your children. Think about it. First, when we see Amnon begging for his sister to come and serve him and he partitions his father David. I just feel like this should have sent up a red flag to David. Why is it that his sister Tamar the only person who can serve him with fidelity? This tragic incident would not have gotten passed David if his relationship with God had not been damaged. The conclusion I keep drawing goes back to lack of true relationship. The relationship I am speak of is with David and his children to include God if David's relationship with God had not been severed or interrupted by the brutal murder that David plotted against Uriah this would have never happened. Now we see David in quite a quandary and now, yet another tragedy has stricken the household of King David.

[30] While they were on the way, news came to David, "Absalom has struck down all the king's sons, and not one of them is left." [31] Then the king arose and [l]tore his garments and [m]lay on the earth. And all his servants who were standing by tore their garments. [32] But [n]Jonadab the son of Shimeah, David's brother, said, "Let not my lord suppose that they have killed all the young men, the king's sons, for Amnon alone is dead. For by the command of Absalom this has been determined from the day he violated his sister Tamar. [33] Now therefore let not my lord the king so [o]take it to heart as to suppose that all the king's sons are dead, for Amnon alone is dead."

Absalom Flees to Geshur

³⁴ ᵖBut Absalom fled. And the young man who kept the watch lifted his eyes and looked, and behold, many people were coming from the road behind him⁵ by the side of the mountain. ³⁵ And Jonadab said to the king, "Behold, the king's sons have come; as your servant said, so it has come about." ³⁶ And as soon as he had finished speaking, behold, the king's sons came and lifted up their voice and wept. And the king also and all his servants wept very bitterly.

³⁷ ᵍBut Absalom fled and went to ʳTalmai the son of Ammihud, king of ˢGeshur. And David mourned for his son day after day. ³⁸ ᵍSo Absalom fled and went to Geshur, and was there three years. ³⁹ And the spirit of the king⁶ longed to go outᶻ to Absalom, because ᵗhe was comforted about Amnon, since he was dead.

Points to Consider: This bitter family tragedy is something not so often taught or preached about for several reasons. My first guess is because we often see David in such a glories light. David is also view as a Christ like example in many cases. We do know that Christ Jesus in born through the linage of King David. We also know that God states that he is a man after his own heart. These accolades places people at a point where they may not be able to have quality conversations on these topics or they just choose to stay away from them for whatever reason they choose to.

I chose to share these things because I believe it is a clear indication of how families who lack quality relationships with one another and most importantly with God can cause mass chaos to this degree and even higher. I further believe of the importance of fully understanding the importance in our actions and how they affect our families and the people around us. We as people must understand the consequences of our actions are not limited to us and us alone. Our consequences can directly impact our children and our children's children. David's children were suffering consequences of his actions. David was far told that the sword would not leave his house. These examples show how powerful Gods word is.

I hope the take away from this is that Gods judgement for David or for us runs much deeper than we have the capacity to understand. Often as adults we say I am grown I can do whatever I feel like doing and or stay out of my business. I believe this is a defensive mechanism use by offended people to get us to just leave them alone and stay out of their businesses or affairs. Affairs they protect and do not want people to get involved or disturb.

I hope to hear this tragic story about David allows us to see the impact one wrong decision can have on the entire family. My goal is not to turn you off or away from David's phenomenal life but to teach you how not to have this happen to you or your children.

We see David as a mighty warrior, musician and poet who seeks to do Gods biding with fidelity, but we often overlook his adulterous affair and how he directly plots to cover it up. When David's plan is spoiled, I believe by divine intervention David seeks to take a man's wife and his life and follows through with it. We hear of how he takes Uriah's wife in a very uncommon way and she becomes pregnant. We see him desperately working to right a wrong with gimmicks and tricks. The way he tries to justify his wrong doing is very deceitful and God is not pleased with the end results. We see the outcomes of God's displeasure in David's past wrong doings and as a result he loses a son physically to death another mentally and emotionally as a result of killing his own brother and in essence he loses a daughter to rape and mental anguish. David loses three sons and a daughter for his adulterous and murderous actions. I strongly believe that if he had not taken the life of Uriah none of this would have happen. We see Uriah's love and dedication to his King and his country as unparalleled and as a result understand Gods actions toward his servant king.

CHAPTER 8

LEAGUE OF EXTRAORDINARY GENTLEMEN

David's Mighty Men

Points to Consider: We often hear of mighty men of valor and great exploits in our history books and even in the bible but there are so many that actually get lost in nonfiction therefore I wanted to highlight just a few extra ordinary individuals that are often overlooked, not mention and rarely spoke of. I believe that their actions are superior and if the bible makes mention of them so should I. There is not a lot of information about these gentlemen other than they won enormous victories along with King David by the power of God.

Josheb-basshebeth a Tahchemonite

⁸ These are the names of the mighty men whom David had: ˢ**Josheb-basshebeth** a Tahchemonite; he was chief of the three.ˢ He wielded his spearᶜ against eight hundred whom he killed at one time. ⁹ And next to him among the three mighty men was **Eleazar** the son of ᵗDodo, son of ᵘAhohi. He was with David when they defied the Philistines who were gathered there for battle, and the men of Israel withdrew. ¹⁰ He rose and struck down the Philistines until his hand was weary, and his hand clung to the sword. And the LORD brought about a great victory that day, and the men returned after him only to strip the slain.

Points to Consider: Josheb-basshebeth a Tahchemonite; he was chief of the three and the wisest. This speaks volume about the character and abilities of Tahchemonite to be the wisest of this league of extraordinary gentlemen that fought for and alongside of King David. The second and possible one of the most successful kings to ever rule. David was a solider from his youth killing the giant Goliath when he was just a boy. David was a very brave warrior for the Lord. David loved and cherished God. Therefore, the men we speak in this section had to have a special bond with their king. I chose to coin this chapter after a movie that was filled with men who were gifted with extra special talents. The movie was very exciting and action pack. The movie was filled with battles and unique undertakings just like David's mighty men. This story was an amazing story and one that everyone should be fully aware of. Tahchemonite the chief of the three men I will mention here phenomenal to say the least. He wielded his spear against eight hundred whom he killed at one time. This is so amazing that it is almost impossible to even believe. Can you imagine one man being so filled with Gods power that he defeats 800 men? The only other story in the bible like this is the story of Samson. Of course, most people who study the bible or went to Sunday school are familiar with Samson and his strength. Until now I have never been able to discover anyone who comes close to this type of victory outside of Samson. In case you are not familiar with the story of Samson here is a snap shot. The story of Samson can be found in Judges 15 and it goes like this, finding a fresh **jawbone** of a donkey, he grabbed it and struck down a thousand **men.** Then **Samson said,** "With a donkey's **jawbone** I have made donkeys of them. With a donkey's **jawbone** I have **killed** a thousand **men.**" When he finished speaking, he threw away the **jawbone;** and the place was called Ramath Lehi. So, what we discover is yet another man of God to whom we are not that familiar with other than being one of King David's warriors we do not know much about him other than this enormous victory. The one thing I can say is to be compare to Samson is amazing. He killed 200 less men with a spear and you probably never even heard of him until know.

Shammah, the son of Agee the ᵛHararite

[11] And next to him was Shammah, the son of Agee the ᵛHararite. The Philistines gathered together at Lehi,ᶻ where there was a plot of ground full of lentils, and the men fled from the Philistines. [12] But he took his stand in the midst of the plot and defended it and struck down the Philistines, and the Lᴏʀᴅ worked a great victory. [13] And three of the thirty chief men went down and came about harvest time to David at the ʷcave of Adullam, when a band of Philistines was encamped ˣin the Valley of Rephaim. [14] David was then ʸin the stronghold, and ᶻthe garrison of the Philistines was then at Bethlehem. [15] And David said longingly, "Oh, that someone would give me water to drink from the well of Bethlehem that is by the gate!" [16] Then the three mighty men broke through the camp of the Philistines and drew water out of the well of Bethlehem that was by the gate and carried and brought it to David. But he would not drink of it. He poured it out to the Lᴏʀᴅ [17] and said, "Far be it from me, O Lᴏʀᴅ, that I should do this. Shall I drink ᵃthe blood of the men who went at the risk of their lives?" Therefore he would not drink it. These things the three mighty men did.

[18] Now Abishai, the brother of Joab, the son of Zeruiah, was chief of the thirty.⁸ And he wielded his spear against three hundred men⁹ and killed them and won a name beside the three. [19] He was the most renowned of the thirty¹⁰ and became their commander, but he did not attain to ᵇthe three.

[20] And ᶜBenaiah the son of Jehoiada was a valiant man¹¹ of ᵈKabzeel, a doer of great deeds. He struck down two ariels¹² of Moab. He also went

down and struck down a lion in a pit on a day when snow had fallen. [21] And he struck down an Egyptian, a handsome man. The Egyptian had a spear in his hand, but Benaiah went down to him with a staff and snatched the spear out of the Egyptian's hand and killed him with his own spear. [22] These things did Benaiah the son of Jehoiada, and won a name beside the three mighty men. [23] He was renowned among the thirty, but he did not attain to the three. And David set him over his bodyguard.

CHAPTER 9

THE IMPACT OF A WISE FATHER TO HIS SON IS UNMEASURABLE

Points to Consider: There is such an important role that fathers play in the life of their children in these next few chapters of King David, King Solomon and other kings we see the impact to following the wisdom of your father and the consequences of not doing so until the end. We will discover that like our friends we often follow that we can become victims of our own circumstances so through these next few texts I will allow you to read and study the word of God. The reading will be easy and self-explanatory

David's Instructions to Solomon

2 *n*When David's time to die drew near, he commanded Solomon his son, saying, ² *o*"I am about to go the way of all the earth. *p*Be strong, and show yourself a man, ³ and keep the charge of the LORD your God, walking in his ways and keeping his statutes, his commandments, his rules, and his testimonies, as it is written in the Law of Moses, *q*that you may prosper in all that you do and wherever you turn, ⁴ that the LORD may *r*establish his word that he spoke concerning me, saying, *s*"If your sons pay close attention to their way, *t*to walk before me in faithfulness with all their heart and with all their soul, *u*you shall not lack*L* a man on the throne of Israel.' ¹⁰ *v*Then David slept with his fathers and was buried in *t*the city of David. ¹¹ And the time that David reigned over Israel was

*j*forty years. He reigned seven years in Hebron and thirty-three years in Jerusalem. [12] *k*So Solomon sat on the throne of David his father, and his kingdom was firmly established.

Points to Consider: This is information that every father should impart to his son before leaving this earth if given the opportunity to do so. This advice is amazing and true, and we will see the outcome of when he follows it and what happens when strays away from it.

Solomon's Prayer for Wisdom

3 [3] Solomon *h*loved the Lord, *c*walking in the statutes of David his father, only he sacrificed and made offerings at the high places. [4] And the king went to Gibeon to sacrifice there, *d*for that was the great high place. Solomon used to offer a thousand burnt offerings on that altar. [5] *e*At Gibeon *f*the Lord appeared to Solomon *g*in a dream by night, and God said, "Ask what I shall give you." [6] And Solomon said, "You have shown great and steadfast love to your servant David my father, because *h*he walked before you in faithfulness, in righteousness, and in uprightness of heart toward you. And you have kept for him this great and steadfast love and *i*have given him a son to sit on his throne this day. [7] And now, O Lord my God, *j*you have made your servant king in place of David my father, *k*although I am but a little child. I do not know *l*how to go out or come in. [8] *m*And your servant is in the midst of your people whom you have chosen, a great people, *n*too many to be numbered or counted for multitude. [9] *o*Give your servant therefore an understanding mind *p*to govern your people, that I may *q*discern between good and evil, for who is able to govern this your great people?"

[10] It pleased the Lord that Solomon had asked this. [11] And God said to him, "Because you have asked this, and have not asked for yourself long life or riches or the life of your enemies, but have asked for yourself

understanding to discern what is right, [12] behold, [I now do according to your word. Behold, [I give you a wise and discerning mind, so that none like you has been before you and none like you shall arise after you. [13] [I give you also what you have not asked, [both riches and honor, so that no other king shall compare with you, all your days. [14] And if you will walk in my ways, keeping my statutes and my commandments, [as your father David walked, then [I will lengthen your days."

[15] And Solomon [awoke, and behold, it was a dream. Then he came to Jerusalem and stood before the ark of the covenant of the Lord, and offered up burnt offerings and peace offerings, and made a feast for all his servants.

Points to Consider: We see him continuing to follow in the wise counsel of his father King David and the benefits that come along with following what has be established with in him. The problem comes when he no longer has the capacity to follow what was established within him from his father. A man coined after Gods own heart.

Solomon's Wisdom

[16] Then two prostitutes came to the king [and stood before him. [17] The one woman said, "Oh, my lord, this woman and I live in the same house, and I gave birth to a child while she was in the house. [18] Then on the third day after I gave birth, this woman also gave birth. And we were alone. There was no one else with us in the house; only we two were in the house. [19] And this woman's son died in the night, because she lay on him. [20] And she arose at midnight and took my son from beside me, while your servant slept, and laid him at her breast, and laid her dead son at my breast. [21] When I rose in the morning to nurse my child, behold, he was dead. But when I looked at him closely in the morning, behold, he was not the child that I had borne." [22] But the other woman said, "No,

the living child is mine, and the dead child is yours." The first said, "No, the dead child is yours, and the living child is mine." Thus they spoke before the king.

²³ Then the king said, "The one says, 'This is my son that is alive, and your son is dead'; and the other says, 'No; but your son is dead, and my son is the living one.' " ²⁴ And the king said, "Bring me a sword." So a sword was brought before the king. ²⁵ And the king said, "Divide the living child in two, and give half to the one and half to the other." ²⁶ Then the woman whose son was alive said to the king, because ᶻher heart yearned for her son, "Oh, my lord, give her the living child, and by no means put him to death." But the other said, "He shall be neither mine nor yours; divide him." ²⁷ Then the king answered and said, "Give the living child to the first woman, and by no means put him to death; she is his mother." ²⁸ And all Israel heard of the judgment that the king had rendered, and they stood in awe of the king, because they perceived that ᵃthe wisdom of God was in him to do justice.

Points to Consider: We see the wisdom that God has bestowed upon Solomon and the impact it has had not only on him but his people and all the kingdom's and countries he is affiliated with. With this type of power and wisdom how could he allow anything, and anyone come between what God has established in him.

Solomon Turns from the LORD

11 Now ᵘKing Solomon loved many foreign women, along with the daughter of Pharaoh: Moabite, Ammonite, Edomite, Sidonian, and Hittite women, ² from the nations concerning which the LORD had said to the people of Israel, ˣ"You shall not enter into marriage with them, neither shall they with you, for surely they will turn away your heart after their gods." Solomon clung to these in love. ³ He had 700 wives, who were princesses, and 300 concubines. And his wives turned away his heart. [4] For when Solomon was old his wives turned away his heart after other gods, and ˣhis heart was not wholly true to the Lᴏʀᴅ his God, ᶻas was the heart of David his father. [5] For Solomon went after ᵃAshtoreth the goddess of the Sidonians, and after ᵇMilcom the abomination of the Ammonites. [6] So Solomon did what was evil in the sight of the Lᴏʀᴅ and did not wholly follow the Lᴏʀᴅ, as David his father had done. [7] Then Solomon built a high place for ᶜChemosh the abomination of Moab, and for ᵈMolech the abomination of the Ammonites, on the mountain east of Jerusalem. [8] And so he did for all his foreign wives, who made offerings and sacrificed to their gods.

The Lᴏʀᴅ Raises Adversaries

[9] And the Lᴏʀᴅ was angry with Solomon, because ᵉhis heart had turned away from the Lᴏʀᴅ, the God of Israel, ᶠwho had appeared to him twice [10] and ᵍhad commanded him concerning this thing, that he should not go after other gods. But he did not keep what the Lᴏʀᴅ commanded. [11] Therefore the Lᴏʀᴅ said to Solomon, "Since this has been your practice and you have not kept my covenant and my statutes that I have commanded you, ʰI will surely tear the kingdom from you and will give it to your servant. [12] Yet for the sake of David your father I will not do it in your days, but I will tear it out of the hand of your son. [13] However, ⁱI will not tear away all the kingdom, but ʲI will give one tribe to your son, for the sake of David my servant and for the sake of Jerusalem ᵏthat I have chosen."

[14] And the Lᴏʀᴅ raised up an adversary against Solomon, Hadad the Edomite. He was of the royal house in Edom. [15] For ˡwhen David was in Edom, and Joab the commander of the army went up to bury the slain, he struck down every male in Edom [16] (for Joab and all Israel remained there six months, until he had cut off every male in Edom). [17] But Hadad

fled to Egypt, together with certain Edomites of his father's servants,
Hadad still being a little child. 18 They set out from Midian and came
to [m]Paran and took men with them from Paran and came to Egypt, to
Pharaoh king of Egypt, who gave him a house and assigned him an
allowance of food and gave him land. 19 And Hadad found great favor
in the sight of Pharaoh, so that he gave him in marriage the sister of his
own wife, the sister of Tahpenes the queen. 20 And the sister of Tahpenes
bore him Genubath his son, whom Tahpenes weaned in Pharaoh's house.
And Genubath was in Pharaoh's house among the sons of Pharaoh. 21
But when Hadad heard in Egypt [n]that David slept with his fathers and
that Joab the commander of the army was dead, Hadad said to Pharaoh,
"Let me depart, that I may go to my own country." 22 But Pharaoh said
to him, "What have you lacked with me that you are now seeking to go
to your own country?" And he said to him, "Only let me depart."

23 God also raised up as an adversary to him, Rezon the son of Eliada,
who had fled from his master [o]Hadadezer king of Zobah. 24 And he
gathered men about him and became leader of a marauding band, [p]after
the killing by David. And they went to Damascus and lived there and
made him king in Damascus. 25 He was an adversary of Israel all the
days of Solomon, doing harm as Hadad did. And he loathed Israel and
reigned over Syria.

26 [q]Jeroboam the son of Nebat, [r]an Ephraimite of Zeredah, a servant of
Solomon, whose mother's name was Zeruah, a widow, also [s]lifted up
his hand against the king. 27 And this was the reason why he lifted up
his hand against the king. [t]Solomon built the Millo, and closed up the
breach of the city of David his father. 28 The man Jeroboam was very
able, and when Solomon saw that the young man was industrious he
gave him charge over all the forced labor of the house of Joseph. 29 And
at that time, when Jeroboam went out of Jerusalem, the prophet [u]Ahijah
the Shilonite found him on the road. Now Ahijah had dressed himself

in a new garment, and the two of them were alone in the open country. ³⁰ Then Ahijah laid hold of the new garment that was on him, ᵛand tore it into twelve pieces. ³¹ And he said to Jeroboam, "Take for yourself ten pieces, for thus says the LORD, the God of Israel, 'Behold, ᵚI am about to tear the kingdom from the hand of Solomon and will give you ten tribes ³² (but ˣhe shall have one tribe, for the sake of my servant David and for the sake of Jerusalem, ʸthe city that I have chosen out of all the tribes of Israel), ³³ because they haveⁱ forsaken me ᶻand worshiped Ashtoreth the goddess of the Sidonians, Chemosh the god of Moab, and Milcom the god of the Ammonites, and they have not walked in my ways, doing what is right in my sight and keeping my statutes and my rules, as David his father did. ³⁴ Nevertheless, I will not take the whole kingdom out of his hand, but I will make him ruler all the days of his life, for the sake of David my servant whom I chose, who kept my commandments and my statutes. ³⁵ ᵃBut I will take the kingdom out of his son's hand and will give it to you, ten tribes. ³⁶ Yet to his son ˣI will give one tribe, that David my servant may always have ᵇa lamp before me in Jerusalem, ʸthe city where I have chosen to put my name. ³⁷ And I will take you, and you shall reign over all that your soul desires, and you shall be king over Israel. ³⁸ And if you will listen to all that I command you, and will walk in my ways, and do what is right in my eyes by keeping my statutes and my commandments, as David my servant did, ᶜI will be with you and ᵈwill build you a sure house, as I built for David, and I will give Israel to you. ³⁹ And I will afflict the offspring of David because of this, but not forever.' " ⁴⁰ Solomon sought therefore to kill Jeroboam. But Jeroboam arose and fled into Egypt, to ᵉShishak king of Egypt, and was in Egypt until the death of Solomon.

⁴¹ ᶠNow the rest of the acts of Solomon, and all that he did, and his wisdom, are they not written in the Book of the Acts of Solomon? ⁴² And the time that Solomon reigned in Jerusalem over all Israel was forty

years. ⁴³ And Solomon ^gslept with his fathers and was buried in the city of David his father. And ^hRehoboam his son reigned in his place.

Rehoboam's Folly

12 ⁱRehoboam went to ^jShechem, for all Israel had come to Shechem to make him king. ² And as soon as ^kJeroboam the son of Nebat heard of it (for ^lhe was still in Egypt, where he had fled from King Solomon), then Jeroboam returned from^L Egypt. ³ And they sent and called him, and Jeroboam and all the assembly of Israel came and said to Rehoboam, ⁴ ^m"Your father made our yoke heavy. Now therefore lighten the hard service of your father and his heavy yoke on us, and we will serve you." ⁵ He said to them, ⁿ"Go away for three days, then come again to me." So the people went away.

⁶ Then King Rehoboam took counsel with the old men, who had stood before Solomon his father while he was yet alive, saying, "How do you advise me to answer this people?" ⁷ And they said to him, "If you will be a servant to this people today and serve them, and speak good words to them when you answer them, then they will be your servants forever." ⁸ But he abandoned the counsel that the old men gave him and took counsel with the young men who had grown up with him and stood before him. ⁹ And he said to them, "What do you advise that we answer this people who have said to me, 'Lighten the yoke that your father put on us'?" ¹⁰ And the young men who had grown up with him said to him, "Thus shall you speak to this people who said to you, 'Your father made our yoke heavy, but you lighten it for us,' thus shall you say to them, 'My little finger is thicker than my father's thighs. ¹¹ And now, whereas ^mmy father laid on you a heavy yoke, I will add to your yoke. My father disciplined you with whips, but I will discipline you with scorpions.' "

¹² So Jeroboam and all the people came to Rehoboam the third day, as the king said, ᵒ"Come to me again the third day." ¹³ And the king answered the people harshly, and forsaking the counsel that the old men had given him, ¹⁴ he spoke to them according to the counsel of the young men, saying, ᵐ"My father made your yoke heavy, but I will add to your yoke. My father disciplined you with whips, but I will discipline you with scorpions." ¹⁵ So the king did not listen to the people, for ᵖit was a turn of affairs brought about by the LORD that he might fulfill his word, which ᵠthe LORD spoke by Ahijah the Shilonite to Jeroboam the son of Nebat.

The Kingdom Divided

¹⁶ And when all Israel saw that the king did not listen to them, the people answered the king, "What portion do we have in David? We have no inheritance in the son of Jesse. ʳTo your tents, O Israel! Look now to your own house, David." So Israel went to their tents. ¹⁷ But Rehoboam reigned over ˢthe people of Israel who lived in the cities of Judah. ¹⁸ Then King Rehoboam sent ᵗAdoram, who was taskmaster over the forced labor, and all Israel stoned him to death with stones. And King Rehoboam hurried to mount his chariot to flee to Jerusalem. ¹⁹ ᵘSo Israel has been in rebellion against the house of David to this day. ²⁰ And when all Israel heard that Jeroboam had returned, they sent and called him to the assembly and made him king over all Israel. There was none that followed the house of David but ᵛthe tribe of Judah only.

²¹ ʷWhen Rehoboam came to Jerusalem, he assembled all the house of Judah and the tribe of Benjamin, 180,000 chosen warriors, to fight against the house of Israel, to restore the kingdom to Rehoboam the son of Solomon. ²² But the word of God came to ˣShemaiah the man of God: ²³ "Say to Rehoboam the son of Solomon, king of Judah, and to all the house of Judah and Benjamin, and to the ʸrest of the people, ²⁴ 'Thus

says the LORD, You shall not go up or fight against your relatives the people of Israel. Every man return to his home, ²for this thing is from me.' " So they listened to the word of the LORD and went home again, according to the word of the LORD.

Points to Consider: We see another classic case of what happens when someone gets caught up in their feelings. When we follow God's wise counsel everything works out for everyone's good. When we get caught in our feelings like Solomon's son Rehoboam did, lives are forever changed.

CHAPTER 10

KNOW AND LISTEN TO THE VOICE OF GOD AND HIS COMMANDS ONLY

The Prophet's Disobedience

[11] Now [u]an old prophet lived in Bethel. And his sons[l] came and told him all that the man of God had done that day in Bethel. They also told to their father the words that he had spoken to the king. [12] And their father said to them, "Which way did he go?" And his sons showed him the way that the man of God who came from Judah had gone. [13] And he said to his sons, "Saddle the donkey for me." So they saddled the donkey for him and he mounted it. [14] And he went after the man of God and found him sitting under an oak. And he said to him, "Are you the man of God who came from Judah?" And he said, "I am." [15] Then he said to him, "Come home with me and eat bread." [16] And he said, [v]"I may not return with you, or go in with you, neither will I eat bread nor drink water with you in this place, [17] for it was said to me [w]by the word of the LORD, 'You shall neither eat bread nor drink water there, nor return by the way that you came.' " [18] And he said to him, "I also am a prophet as you are, and an angel spoke to me by the word of the LORD, saying, 'Bring him back with you into your house that he may eat bread and drink water.' " But he lied to him. [19] So he went back with him and ate bread in his house and drank water.

²⁰ And as they sat at the table, the word of the LORD came to the prophet who had brought him back. ²¹ And he cried to the man of God who came from Judah, "Thus says the LORD, 'Because you have disobeyed the word of the LORD and have not kept the command that the LORD your God commanded you, ²² but have come back and have eaten bread and drunk water in the place of which he said to you, "Eat no bread and drink no water," your body shall not come to the tomb of your fathers.'" ²³ And after he had eaten bread and drunk, he saddled the donkey for the prophet whom he had brought back. ²⁴ And as he went away ˣa lion met him on the road and killed him. And his body was thrown in the road, and the donkey stood beside it; the lion also stood beside the body. ²⁵ And behold, men passed by and saw the body thrown in the road and the lion standing by the body. And they came and told it in the city where ʸthe old prophet lived.

²⁶ And when the prophet who had brought him back from the way heard of it, he said, "It is the man of God who disobeyed the word of the LORD; therefore the LORD has given him to the lion, which has torn him and killed him, according to the word that the LORD spoke to him." ²⁷ And he said to his sons, "Saddle the donkey for me." And they saddled it. ²⁸ And he went and found his body thrown in the road, and the donkey and the lion standing beside the body. The lion had not eaten the body or torn the donkey. ²⁹ And the prophet took up the body of the man of God and laid it on the donkey and brought it back to the city² to mourn and to bury him. ³⁰ And he laid the body in his own grave. And they mourned over him, saying, ᶻ"Alas, my brother!" ³¹ And after he had buried him, he said to his sons, "When I die, bury me in the grave in which the man of God is buried; ᵃlay my bones beside his bones. ³²ᵇFor the saying that he called out by the word of the LORD against the altar in Bethel and against ᶜall the houses of the high places that are in the cities of ᵈSamaria shall surely come to pass."

Points to Consider: There comes a time in our lives where we are given extremely specific directions from God an in ourselves, we must find confidence in God's word. With the confidence we need to trust God we know that his word is true and will come to pass. We are taught that God is not a man that he can lie nor is he the son of man that he should repent. Knowing these facts and recognizing the unadulterated voice of God validated by the word of God gives us wisdom and power beyond anything man can think or imagine. This next story reveals the importance of obeying and following the voice of God to the very letter. When doing so the outcome is supernaturally remarkable and Gods plan is illustrated in a way that man cannot begin to understand or phantom. God has a plan for his people to be successful and he uses that plan to benefit the lives of his people. However obedience is extremely critical. When we obey Gods words our lives and the countless lives of other people are impacted in an unimaginable way. Let us take a close look at the outcomes of listening to the voice of God and his instructions. In this next story there is an incredibly unique cast of characters. We have a corrupt king leading the people of God named Ahab. You have his wicked wife Jezebel who essentially rules the kingdom despite him being the king. You have Obadiah who is over the Kings household but he feared the Lord Almighty and despite the corrupt king and evil queen Obadiah must serve, he hides and feeds over one hundred prophets of God. In doing so he is in direct disobedience to the king and queen he serves. Obadiah despite his duty to the king and queen he fears the Lord greatly. Much like those of us who may work for evil and wicked people it is important that our loyalty lies with God. Obadiah was in an exceedingly difficult position however every opportunity he shows his true loyalty is to God despite the job he has. Before we judge Obadiah, we must recognize that he strategically place in a compromising position that he may ultimately serve the purpose of God. Therefore when we find ourselves in similar situations to draw off Obadiah's example. I know many of you may not even be familiar with who Obadiah is or ever heard of him before now. My prayer is that from this day and beyond you will recognize his position and overall plan in God's plan for our life.

1Kings 18 **Elijah Confronts Ahab**

18 ᵈAfter many days the word of the LORD came to Elijah, in the third year, saying, "Go, show yourself to Ahab, and I will send rain upon the earth." ² So Elijah went to show himself to Ahab. Now the famine was severe in Samaria. ³ And Ahab called Obadiah, who was ᵉover the household. (Now Obadiah feared the LORD greatly, ⁴ and ᶠwhen Jezebel cut off the prophets of the LORD, Obadiah took a hundred prophets and hid them by fifties in a cave and fed them with bread and water.) ⁵ And Ahab said to Obadiah, "Go through the land to all the springs of water and to all the valleys. Perhaps we may find grass and save the horses and mules alive, and not lose some of the animals." ⁶ So they divided the land between them to pass through it. Ahab went in one direction by himself, and Obadiah went in another direction by himself.

⁷ And as Obadiah was on the way, behold, Elijah met him. And Obadiah recognized him and fell on his face and said, "Is it you, my lord Elijah?" ⁸ And he answered him, "It is I. Go, tell your lord, 'Behold, Elijah is here.' " ⁹ And he said, "How have I sinned, that you would give your servant into the hand of Ahab, to kill me? ¹⁰ ᵍAs the LORD your God lives, there is no nation or kingdom where my lord has not sent to seek you. And when they would say, 'He is not here,' he would take an oath of the kingdom or nation, that they had not found you. ¹¹ And now you

say, 'Go, tell your lord, "Behold, Elijah is here." ' ¹² And as soon as I have gone from you, *the Spirit of the LORD will carry you I know not where. And so, when I come and tell Ahab and he cannot find you, he will kill me, although I your servant have feared the LORD from my youth. ¹³ Has it not been told my lord what I did ʲwhen Jezebel killed the prophets of the LORD, how I hid a hundred men of the LORD's prophets by fifties in a cave and fed them with bread and water? ¹⁴ And now you say, 'Go, tell your lord, "Behold, Elijah is here" '; and he will kill me." ¹⁵ And Elijah said, *"As the LORD of hosts lives, before whom I stand, I will surely show myself to him today." ¹⁶ So Obadiah went to meet Ahab, and told him. And Ahab went to meet Elijah.

¹⁷ When Ahab saw Elijah, Ahab said to him, ʲ"Is it you, you ᵏtroubler of Israel?" ¹⁸ And he answered, "I have not troubled Israel, but you have, and your father's house, because you have ˡabandoned the commandments of the LORD and ᵐfollowed the Baals. ¹⁹ Now therefore send and gather all Israel to me at Mount ⁿCarmel, and the ᵒ450 prophets of Baal and ᵖthe 400 prophets of Asherah, ᵠwho eat at Jezebel's table."

Points to Consider: This is an overly dramatic set of events here. We see irony here were two men with a common purpose come face to face. Elijah and Obadiah the two men fighting for a common cause comes face to face. The text clearly shows that this is there very first time every meeting or meeting one another. The interesting thing is this is way before social media or Facebook Instagram or anything close to that. I mention this because Obadiah only knows of Elijah because King Ahab and Queen Jezebel has been hunting relentlessly for him. Obadiah know this all too well being over there house. I am sure he has been in the room many of times where Elijah's name is constantly coming up in an extremely negative light.

In examining their first interactions we see the overwhelming respect and reverence Obadiah has for Elijah. Obadiah immediately bows down before Elijah and asked the question lord, is it you? Obadiah also recognizes that the directive that Elijah gives him is not one of extreme ease and he speaks very clearly and specifically on the matter. A man after my own heart. He does not just take what the man of God says to heart but he questions his ability to be able to carry out this directive. Obadiah knows all too well that Elijah had been given divine favor from the Lord. He also questions Elijah relationship with God. Obadiah question him by asking him, have not God revealed unto you that it was me who has saved over one hundred prophets of God when King Ahab and Queen Jezebel were seeking them out and killing them all off.

This is a legitimate question and one that must be pointed out. God does not always reveal his full plan, like in this case we really do not know if Elijah has been informed of Obadiah's good deeds or that he has feared the Lord since his youth. What we do know is Elijah does not respond to the question he does give Obadiah his word that he will be available to meet with King Ahab. This confirmation does give him the confident he needs to carry out Elijah's command. At least he now knows the command will not be to the death of him. Because Elijah was known for being exceedingly difficult to detain because of the divine protection of God.

The meeting takes place and King Ahab meets with the man of God. When Ahab saw Elijah, Ahab said to him, [j]"Is it you, you [k]troubler of Israel?" **18** And he answered, "I have not troubled Israel, but you have, and your father's house, because you have [l]abandoned the commandments of the Lord and [m]followed the Baals. **19** Now therefore send and gather all Israel to me at Mount [n]Carmel, and the [o]450 prophets of Baal and [p]the 400 prophets of Asherah, [q]who eat at Jezebel's table."

CHAPTER 11

ONE LORD AND HE IS THE GOD OF THE UNIVERSE

Points to Consider: There has been a difference of opinion for thousands of years about is there a God and or whose God is the most powerful God. Still to this day there is tons of controversy over this topic. I am not sure how many readers have had the opportunity to read this remarkable story. This next chapter of scripture reveal a public show down. This show down of whose God is the real God.

The Prophets of Baal Defeated

[20] So Ahab sent to all the people of Israel and gathered the prophets together at Mount Carmel. [21] And Elijah came near to all the people and said, "How long ʳwill you go limping between two different opinions? ˢIf the Lᴏʀᴅ is God, follow him; but if Baal, then follow him." And the people did not answer him a word. [22] Then Elijah said to the people, ᵗ"I, even I only, am left a prophet of the Lᴏʀᴅ, but Baal's prophets are ᵘ450 men. [23] Let two bulls be given to us, and let them choose one bull for themselves and cut it in pieces and lay it on the wood, but put no fire to it. And I will prepare the other bull and lay it on the wood and put no fire to it. [24] And you call upon the name of your god, and I will call upon the name of the Lᴏʀᴅ, and the God who ᵛanswers by fire, he is God." And all the people answered, "It is well spoken." [25] Then Elijah said to the prophets of Baal, "Choose for yourselves one bull and prepare it first,

for you are many, and call upon the name of your god, but put no fire to it." ²⁶ And they took the bull that was given them, and they prepared it and called upon the name of Baal from morning until noon, saying, "O Baal, answer us!" But there was no voice, and no one answered. And they limped around the altar that they had made. ²⁷ And at noon Elijah mocked them, saying, "Cry aloud, for he is a god. Either he is musing, or he is relieving himself, or he is on a journey, or perhaps he is asleep and must be awakened." ²⁸ And they cried aloud and ʷcut themselves after their custom with swords and lances, until the blood gushed out upon them. ²⁹ And as midday passed, they raved on until the time of ˣthe offering of the oblation, but there was no voice. No one answered; no one paid attention.

³⁰ Then Elijah said to all the people, "Come near to me." And all the people came near to him. And he repaired the altar of the LORD that had been ʸthrown down. ³¹ Elijah took twelve stones, according to the number of the tribes of the sons of Jacob, to whom the word of the LORD came, saying, ᶻ"Israel shall be your name," ³² and with the stones he built an altar in the name of the LORD. And he made a trench about the altar, as great as would contain two seahsˡ of seed. ³³ ᵃAnd he put the wood in order and cut the bull in pieces and laid it on the wood. And he said, "Fill four jars with water and ᵇpour it on the burnt offering and on the wood." ³⁴ And he said, "Do it a second time." And they did it a second time. And he said, "Do it a third time." And they did it a third time. ³⁵ And the water ran around the altar and filled the trench also with water.

³⁶ And at the time of ᶜthe offering of the oblation, Elijah the prophet came near and said, "O LORD, ᵈGod of Abraham, Isaac, and Israel, let it be known this day that ᵉyou are God in Israel, and that I am your servant, and that ᶠI have done all these things at your word. ³⁷ Answer me, O LORD, answer me, that this people may know that you, O LORD, are God, and that you have turned their hearts back." ³⁸ ᵍThen the fire

of the LORD fell and consumed the burnt offering and the wood and the stones and the dust, and licked up the water that was in the trench. [39] And when all the people saw it, they fell on their faces and said, [h]"The LORD, he is God; the LORD, he is God." [40] And Elijah said to them, "Seize the prophets of Baal; let not one of them escape." And they seized them. And Elijah brought them down to [i]the brook Kishon and [j]slaughtered them there.

The LORD Sends Rain

[41] And Elijah said to Ahab, "Go up, eat and drink, for there is a sound of the rushing of rain." [42] So Ahab went up to eat and to drink. And Elijah went up to the top of Mount Carmel. [k]And he bowed himself down on the earth and put his face between his knees. [43] And he said to his servant, "Go up now, look toward the sea." And he went up and looked and said, "There is nothing." And he said, "Go again," seven times. [44] And at the seventh time he said, "Behold, [l]a little cloud like a man's hand is rising from the sea." And he said, "Go up, say to Ahab, 'Prepare your chariot and go down, lest the rain stop you.' " [45] And in a little while the heavens grew black with clouds and wind, and there was a great rain. And Ahab rode and went to [m]Jezreel. [46] [n]And the hand of the LORD was on Elijah, [o]and he gathered up his garment and ran before Ahab to the entrance of [p]Jezreel.

Elijah Flees Jezebel

19 Ahab told Jezebel all that Elijah had done, and how [q]he had killed all the prophets with the sword. [2] Then Jezebel sent a messenger to Elijah, saying, [r]"So may the gods do to me and more also, if I do not make your life as the life of one of them by this time tomorrow." [3] Then he was afraid, and he arose and ran for his life and came to [s]Beersheba, which belongs to Judah, and left his servant there.

⁴ But he himself went a day's journey into the wilderness and came and sat down under a broom tree. ᶦAnd he asked that he might die, saying, "It is enough; now, O LORD, take away my life, for I am no better than my fathers." ⁵ And he lay down and slept under a broom tree. And behold, an angel touched him and said to him, "Arise and eat." ⁶ And he looked, and behold, there was at his head a cake baked on hot stones and a jar of water. And he ate and drank and lay down again. ⁷ And the angel of the LORD came again a second time and touched him and said, "Arise and eat, for the journey is too great for you." ⁸ And he arose and ate and drank, and went in the strength of that food ᵘforty days and forty nights to ᵛHoreb, the mount of God.

Points to Consider: This has always been one of my favorite bible stories; however it has always been puzzling to me as to how Elijah finds himself in this position. Elijah has just completed one of the greatest victories known to man. He defeats over 800 false prophets of Baal in a single setting. Who would imagine after such a great victory given to him by God that he would allow such a simple message to render him so fearful that he becomes powerless? Jezebel does not come on her own but she simply sends a message. A message that completely shatters his victory, understanding of who God is, and the power of God. How can anyone begin to explain how this could happen so quickly after such a great victory? Surely if God did it one time, he would do it again.

For years, this situation was completely puzzling to me until one day the Holy Spirit revealed that just like Elijah any man could find himself in this position out of fear. Fear has and unexplainable power. Fear can render the greatest of men and women to find themselves in a crippling and powerless state of being. I used to judge Elijah to some degree as a coward and a failure. Reason being is because for some unknown reason to me, I simply could not understand how this could happen to a man of God who calls down fire from heaven slays over 800 hundred false prophets

. One day I was reading in the scriptures that as soon as the word of the Lord comes the enemy of the Lord comes to steal it away. According to Mark 4:15 (AMP) these (in the first group) are the ones along the road where the word is sown, but when hear, Satan immediately comes and takes away the word which has been sown in them. I bring this important part up because during this time and season, men and women of God did not have the Holy Spirit; however, God still used them mightily. Recognizing that the Holy Spirit did not dwell inside of them makes it extremely clear to me as to why Elijah became so frightened. We must be mindful as the spirit of God anything is subject to happen. During the time of this great victory, Elijah called on God's presence the difference is having to call on the God as opposed to having God living in you. Case in point: Post Holy Spirit we should never find ourselves in this position because we do not have to call on God because he already lives in us. One especially important tip is, we still must activate the Holy Spirit that lives in us in order to activate the word of God. Without immediate activation of the Holy Spirit we too will find ourselves be in the same position as Elijah was.

Points to Consider: Elijah is so fearful that he runs for his life and he runs over 100 miles to get away from Jezebel. Wow that is so unbelievable for someone to be so afraid that they have run so far. Let's look at his run-in terms of using a vehicle traveling at least 70 miles an hour. To drive 100 miles in a car, it is about an hour and 30 minutes alone. According to scripture, Jezreel to Beersheba is over a hundred miles. I noticed he leaves his servant and travels another whole day by himself.

I also wondered why he left his servant and travel alone. Two things come to mind immediately; the enemy encourages us to separate one from another so that there are no outside influences when our thinking is off. When we come to our last mile, there are times when we do not want anyone to go down the dark paths we are traveling. We see he travels another day's journey alone. He finally stops and rest.

When we are extremely exhausted and tired our thinking is off. We find Elijah at the lowest point of his journey. He is exhausted, alone and extremely confused. A perfect combination for the enemy to enter in to steal, kill, and destroy. Like Elijah some of us have found ourselves in similar conditions where we wanted to give up on everything we know and believe to be true. This state of mine is never extremely far away from ones thinking.

We see God comes to his rescue providing simple but critical aid in the form of food and water. The food and water provide replenishing his natural body. Initially I did not understand why God would take the time and provide him with food and water and let him rest. I now clearly understand that God was ministering to his physical needs. I am not sure if we would have the wisdom or compassion to recognize this need and meet it. Without it we cannot think properly and God knew and understood this. It is extremely important to note that God not only feeds him once but he does it twice. God know what we have need of and when we need it, God supplies it.

I noticed God does not attempt to speak to him about the detrimental things that he had spoken while exhausted. Wow what an amazing God who would not serve a God like this. God knows and understands just where he was mentally emotionally and physically. Elijah's thoughts are I am all alone and he speaks out of his mouth I am no better than my father's let me die. Wow his talking like a mad man who has never followed or had a relationship with God. These are all things Elijah spoke while exhausted.

God does not address these things. He simply provides for Elijah's immediate needs. Let us remember Elijah has been running for 48 straight hours all out of fear. The fear he had was out of a mere gesture from Jezebel's wicked mind. The question remains why this simple gesture from Jezebel causes him so much grief, stress, and fear. One main fact is Jezebel had a very harsh repetition and she was known to kill the prophets of God with no remorse.

Elijah feels completely alone and despite his long relationship with God, feels the time is now come for him to hang up his hat and die. I love how God responds to our emotions. God's first response was to meet his natural needs. God's second response was to meet his natural needs. God utterly understands and recognizes having a conversation with Elijah during his time of great need and overall fear would be useless.

Points to Consider: When trying to minister to people and win souls to Christ meet them where they are. People cannot receive anything from you or me when there is an overwhelming need being food, shelter, or some other need on Maslow's hierarchy of needs. Please do not quote scriptures to someone who is in dire need. There is more to Ministry than quoting scriptures.

God reveals an especially important fact for us here with this example with Elijah. Please do not miss this important note. God addresses Elijah's concern after Elijah's needs are thoroughly met. Elijah has eaten twice and he has rested well before God ministers to him. Remember Elijah felt alone and he expressed this to God. God directly answers his question with a simple statement. The statement was I have 7000 prophets who have never bowed down to Baal. What I hear God saying in this statement is Elijah get it together you are not alone. I have 7000 who have never bowed down to Balaam so what are you talking about.

The LORD Speaks to Elijah

⁹ There he came to a cave and lodged in it. And behold, ᵘthe word of the LORD came to him, and he said to him, "What are you doing here, Elijah?" ¹⁰ He said, "I have been very ˣjealous for the LORD, the God of hosts. For the people of Israel have forsaken your covenant, ʸthrown down your altars, and ᶻkilled your prophets with the sword, ᵃand I, even I only, am left, and they seek my life, to take it away." ¹¹ And he said, "Go

out and ^bstand on the mount before the Lord." And behold, the Lord passed by, and ^ca great and strong wind tore the mountains and broke in pieces the rocks before the Lord, but the Lord was not in the wind. And after the wind ^dan earthquake, but the Lord was not in the earthquake. ¹² And after the earthquake a fire, but the Lord was not in the fire. And after the fire the sound of a low whisper.^l ¹³ And when Elijah heard it, ^ehe wrapped his face in his cloak and went out and stood at the entrance of the cave. And behold, ^fthere came a voice to him and said, "What are you doing here, Elijah?" ¹⁴ He said, ^x"I have been very jealous for the Lord, the God of hosts. For the people of Israel have forsaken your covenant, ^ythrown down your altars, and killed your prophets with the sword, and I, even I only, am left, and they seek my life, to take it away." ¹⁵ And the Lord said to him, "Go, return on your way to the wilderness of Damascus. And when you arrive, you shall anoint Hazael to be king over Syria. ¹⁶ ^gAnd Jehu the son of Nimshi you shall anoint to be king over Israel, and ^hElisha the son of Shaphat of Abel-meholah you shall anoint to be prophet in your place. ¹⁷ And the one who escapes from ⁱthe sword of Hazael ^jshall Jehu put to death, and the one who escapes from the sword of Jehu ^kshall Elisha put to death. ¹⁸ ^lYet I will leave seven thousand in Israel, all the knees that have not bowed to Baal, and every mouth that has not ^mkissed him."

CHAPTER 12

THE UNHINGING LOVE OF GOD

Points to Consider: Have you ever been in a place in your life where you felt all alone as if you there was no one to call on in a time of help or great need? I believe it is safe to say that a large percentage of us have felt that way one way or another. I am reminded of the poem footsteps in the sand. The poem goes on to talk about when times were good there were two sets of foot prints in the sand and when times get ruff there were only one set of foot prints. In the story the question asked of God why is that when things became rough, I could only see one set of foot prints in the sand. In the mind of the individual he believes that during this time God was not with them. Therefore he asked the question why there is only one set of prints in the sand. God said it is during this time I carried you because you were not able to walk. The moral of the story is that we cannot always feel or recognize God at work but trust and believe God does not sleep nor does he slumber. God say no man can pluck you out of my hands. This is true but we can take ourselves out of Gods hand based on our action's choices or decisions. Choose God this day for he will take care of you.

This next story was selected for the reasoning and understanding that God is always working on our behalf because he loves us unconditionally. The man of God believe that he is all alone and we see God coming in to rescued him and take care of him. This also a great example of listening and following Gods commands. This story reveals how not only was the man of God bless but the widow woman who was in a desperate place is provided for as well. This encourages me to always remember that no matter what things feel like or how I perceive things God is there fighting on my behalf and even though I may not readily understand God is right there by my side fighting my battles. Who would not serve a God like this?

1 Kings 17
The Widow of Zarephath

8Then the word of the LORD came to Elijah: **9**"Get up and go to Zarephath of Sidon, and stay there. Behold, I have commanded a widow there to provide for you."

10So Elijah got up and went to Zarephath. When he arrived at the city gate, there was a widow gathering sticks. Elijah called to her and said, "Please bring me a little water in a cup, so that I may drink." **11**And as she was going to get it, he called to her and said, "Please bring me a piece of bread."

12But she replied, "As surely as the LORD your God lives, I have no bread—only a handful of flour in a jar and a little oil in a jug. Look, I am gathering a couple of sticks to take home and prepare a meal for myself and my son, so that we may eat it and die."

13"Do not be afraid," Elijah said to her. "Go and do as you have said. But first make me a small cake of bread from what you have, and bring it out to me. Afterward, make some for yourself and your son, **14**for this is what the LORD, the God of Israel, says: 'The jar of flour will not be exhausted and the jug of oil will not run dry until the day the LORD sends rain upon the face of the earth.'"

15So she went and did according to the word of Elijah, and there was food every day for Elijah and the woman and her household. **16**The jar of flour was not exhausted and the jug of oil did not run dry, according to the word that the LORD had spoken through Elijah.

CHAPTER 13

A WORD OF ENCOURAGEMENT: DURING A TIME OF PANDEMIC, POLITICAL, SOCIAL AND CIVIL UNREST.

A Relevant word of Encouragement to the church from my heart to yours

Luke 17

Then said he unto the disciples, it is impossible but that offences will come but woe unto him, through whom they come!

2 It were better for him that a millstone were hanged about his neck, and he cast into the sea, than that he should offend one of these little ones.

3 Take heed to yourselves: If thy brother trespass against thee, rebuke him; and if he repent, forgive him.

4 And if he trespass against thee seven times in a day, and seven times in a day turn again to thee, saying, I repent; thou shalt forgive him.

5 And the apostles said unto the Lord, Increase our faith.

6 And the Lord said, If ye had faith as a grain of mustard seed, ye might say unto this sycamine tree, Be thou plucked up by the root, and be thou planted in the sea; and it should obey you.

Col. 3:16)

3:16 Let the word of Christ dwell in you richly, teaching and exhorting one another with all wisdom, singing psalms, hymns, and spiritual songs, all with grace in your hearts to God.

Mathew 28:19-20

28:19 therefore go and make disciples of all nations, baptizing them in the name of the Father and the Son and the Holy Spirit, **20** teaching them to obey everything I have commanded you. And remember, I am with you always, to the end of the age."

1 Peter 1:7

[7] That the trial of your faith, being much more precious than of gold that perished, though it be tried with fire, might be found unto praise and honor and glory at the appearing of Jesus Christ:

What is the State of your church?

The Lord is saying it's time to view the God we serve from a much greater prospective and capacity. Have you ever just closed your eyes and tried to imagine the vast greatness and power in the God we serve? Do you really have a clue or inkling to just how powerful the God of this universe is? I am sure someone is wondering what does this has to do with me? It has everything to do with the church/you and the state of the church. The church is only as powerful as its source. In this case we have and unlimited source of Power in Christ Jesus.

In my experiences I come to believe that there are those of the church who just do not seem to get it. Much like the children of Israel they died not getting it. They saw plague after plague affect their enemy but not them. They saw the red see divided and walked across on dry ground. They feed off manner from heaven daily.

How you view God is everything and if you only see or experience God during times of great need you can only view God from one set of lenses, therefore the church can never meet its full potential on the earth. The church must be healthy and balance that the world may see Christ Jesus through the church. If the world does not see Christ in all his majesty and power, then there is a systemic problem within that individual church. The church should be the light that sit on a hill for the world to see and gleam from. The world should be able to gleam the power of God through the church. When the church functions in this capacity lives are changed, transformed, renewed and set on course to reproduce like kind.

When you look around and you see people are dying daily by the thousands due to this modern-day plague called COVID-19 19 or through senseless killings in a country that has in God we Trust on our money. We now live in a very jaded world where you can no longer do the simple things in life like visit your family, go the movies, or even step into the church building to worship God together. Something that none of us could even imagine happening in our world. Perhaps over in a third world country but not right here in the united states.

So you must ask yourself "What is the state of my church"

If there were ever a time that the world needs to see Christ Jesus through the church is right now. Do not become fearful or delusional because God has not forgotten nor has ever left us. Have you now forgotten the power of God? Let me remind you that plagues have always been around and there is not a plague yet that has defeated Christ Jesus.

The question the church must respond to is what is over your door post? What are the words that are coming out of your mouth? What are the things you allow to entertain your thoughts? Why has God spared your life from this deadly plague when so many have died over 210 thousand American citizens have died and continue to die and even more have been affected and will become effected. Some of us have been directly affected, by the death of friends or family members?

What we are experiencing now was something completely foreign. The church is being attacked by unseen obstacles and man has not a clue as to how to counter act this global crisis. There are those who have been running around like a chicken with its head cut off as if there were no God. These obstacles have over taken some by surprise. There are those who have become hopeless and have forgotten that God still sits on the Thrown. Therefor No Weapon formed against the church of the living God will prosper. Yes, it will form but it will not prosper because of the power in God's word. God very plainly and specifically points out in Mathew that heaven and earth shall pass away but my word will never pass away. Now that's power beyond what most people can imagine.

How Do you view your church?

There are those who have miss understood and continue misunderstand the shear purpose of the church. They have viewed the church from a place it was not meant to be view from.

Ex. 1. The brick and mortar, the chairs, banners, the carpet, and yes, the floor towel and the people inside.

These are all-natural ways of viewing the church, not that there is anything wrong with viewing the church from this prospective, however our faith is designed to propel us beyond the natural and only view things from the natural point of view. Our faith is an extremely critical component to our lives. **Hebrews 11:6, "And without faith it is impossible to please God, because anyone who comes to him must believe that he exists and that he rewards those who earnestly seek him." ... Anyone who wants to come to him must believe that God exists and that he rewards those who sincerely seek him."**

God says without faith it is impossible to please me, and without it no man will see God.

The church is so much greater than what you can see or phantom for my thoughts are not your thoughts my thoughts are so much greater than yours. **Isaiah 55:8-9**

8 "For my thoughts are not your thoughts, neither are your ways my ways,"

declares the Lord. 9 "As the heavens are higher than the earth, so are my ways higher than your ways and my thoughts than your thoughts.

The Power in your thoughts:

The time is out for the saints of the highest God to keep him boxed in to only what you can see with your natural eyes and hear with your natural ears. Do not box me in sayeth the Lord, that time is no longer relevant for you in this season. Therefore it is extremely important to know and fully understand the season you are in. for my people who are called by my name to box me in, or to limit your faith to being boxed in to a building or a location because our God is so much greater than what man can even began to comprehend!

I am a God that cannot be contained in an ark or inside of walls. My reach is greater than what you can see hear or even imagine. I know you do not understand the state of your world that you have grown to love. Therefor even at this very moment I am calling you to a repentance, not for what you think but for what you have not done. You have not allowed me to grow you pass your building, you have kept me confined to four walls of a building, a city with walls, a state with walls. I am who am. I am God and my reach is limitless

Man seek answers to questions that have already been given since the dawn of time for I am not a man said the Lord I am God!

Numbers 23:19God is not human, that he should lie, not a human being, that he should change his mind. Does he speak and then not act? Does he promise and not fulfill?

The church must begin to understand that God is eternal. In understanding that we must then understand that in God there is no beginning and there is no end as men you seek to understand the time the day the hour. Yeah, I say that the time is now for the hour is at hand seek me now while it is still day for there comes a time where you will seek me but you want to be able to find me. You wonder why the doors of the church building have been closed. You wonder why the earth is in Chaos. In these places you have not sought after me with your whole heart. You have sought after popularity, social clubs, and things that have absolutely nothing to do with me or my purpose for your life.

What have you done to change this world for the power of life and death is the tongue what have you spoken? Why do look and gaze, why you pray a hope when you have the power to unleash healing and deliverance. I have already come that you may have life and have life more abundantly. How long will the blood of the living church be on your hands?

You ask how the blood of the living church is on your hands. When did you say to least of them the power of all things is in the hands of God? When did you allow the little ones to come unto me without doubting their sincerity? When did you declare me King of Kings and Lord of Lords in your homes, in your neighborhoods, on yours jobs and yes even in your churches? So as you seek to celebrate this year recognize there is still so much more work to be done. The harvest is plentiful but the labors are few. I say repent and turn from your wicked ways then will I hear from heaven and heal your land. For I am God. You ask yourself where is God that he would allow such tragic things to happen I say where have you been having you been living by your bread alone? For man shall not live by bread alone but by every word that proceeded out of the mouth of God. You do not understand because you have not humbled yourself to minister to me yet you constantly seek me to minister unto you, should not the child return unto the parent that same love and care. Should you not return unto the father that I which I have given unto you for I have loved you from the time you were in your mother's womb? I have been with you in times of happiness and times of uncertainty I have never left you I have always been there for you as I am with you right now in your homes on the phone line, where can you go that I am not there. My presence hovers over you as a doting mother who protects her young as a father who provides protection and certainty in a time of uncertainty.

So as you begin to celebrate man's accomplishment remember from whence, they have derived by whom it has been delivered, manifested, and given power to operate for it is not by man's hands but the Lords. I am the God that your thoughts can not even begin to imagine the power I have place in your hands alone. I say use what is in your hands and speak light to every dark situation you see. Take my word and activate it with the power I have given you and be yeah not afraid for it is I that will guide and direct your path it is I who will protect you against the evil one who has sought to sift you as wheat and destroy your existence but I have spare you that you might be a church Siting on a hill to draw men unto me that the earth would replenish itself and reproduce like kind that you will be a church housed with the love that covers a multitude of sin a church that has compassion for all mankind. A church that still believes all things are possible to them that believe!

Think it not strange that you are doing something new and different something that you could have never imagined before now. Who would have ever imagined in their life time that we would be Celebrating church anniversary over the phone, going to mid-week service on the phone, having prayer meeting over the phone? For all intense purpose we see these things as being very indifferent.

Now look at from the prospective when has the church had the ability to reach people of all ages ethnicity to include family members who cannot or would not necessarily come together on one mind and one accord or on this level to experience God. This phone line was never on anyone's radar prior to COVID-19 19 or this time last year. The phone line was created out of desperation to save and sustain the church that Gods people would not lose hope as man has. God created this form of communication so that God's people would still taste and see the goodness of God. This is not just a phone line ministry but a life line ministry seeking to save souls. This line has provided direction, structure, wisdom, fellowship, and most of all Life in darkness. Now the church's range is much greater reaching people in Texas, Mississippi, South Carolina, Mexico and beyond. In closing I say stay focused keep your eyes set as flint on God, Study Gods word as your life truly does depend on it. I leave you with two important scriptures.

1 Corinthians 1:27

27 But God has chosen the foolish things of the world to put to shame the wise, and God has chosen the weak things of the world to put to shame the things which are mighty.

Psalm 42

1 As the deer pants for streams of water, so my soul pants for you, my God.
2 My soul thirsts for God, for the living God. When can I go and meet with God

Printed in the United States
by Baker & Taylor Publisher Services